Vox

POP CULTURE CROSSWORDS

80 Puzzles for Curious Minds

PUZZLE
WRIGHT
PRESS

New York

PUZZLE
WRIGHT
PRESS
New York

An Imprint of Sterling Publishing Co., Inc.

The puzzles in this book originally appeared on the
Vox.com website between October 2020 and April 2022.

ISBN 978-1-4549-5006-6

For information about custom editions, special sales, and premium purchases,
please contact specialsales@unionsquareandco.com.

Manufactured in Canada

2   4   6   8   10   9   7   5   3   1

unionsquareandco.com

Cover design by Gavin Motnyk
Cover icons, from left: Oldesign/Shutterstock.com; courtesy of Vox Media (×2)

CONTENTS

INTRODUCTION

My mom was a big fan of crosswords. She completed crosswords daily and introduced me to the challenge of a themed Sunday puzzle and the triumph of a completed grid, even with erasures and rewritten words. When I was away at college, she would write me letters sharing a word definition or a particularly groan-worthy pun from a recent L.A. Times puzzle solution. And when I moved to New York, I would clip the puzzles I couldn't finish out of the New York Times and ship the stack across the country for her to complete.

Mom and I are not alone; ever since crosswords debuted in a New York newspaper in 1913, they have proved irresistible. The first book of crosswords was published in 1924 to capture the puzzle-solving public's appetite for the new game, and the New York Times began publishing a Sunday puzzle in 1942 to, in part, give wartime Americans something pleasant to occupy themselves with while sheltering from an air raid. In the decades since, tens of millions of people every day have picked up a pen or pencil or fired up a screen to solve a crossword puzzle.

Vox crosswords, which debuted in October 2019, bring the legacy to another generation of puzzlers; they've become a daily destination for thousands of curious solvers.

This collection of Saturday puzzles provides a range of difficulties and a wealth of themes. Some feature puns, some include anagrams, while still others reference the news or a famous name or a funny word linkage. Vox Saturday puzzles are bigger than the weekday grids and offer a wider scope for creativity. No two are alike, and each will challenge and amuse—and maybe teach you a new word or show you something surprising.

It has been my pleasure to edit these puzzles for the past year, and I couldn't finish this note without thanking the team originally behind the crosswords—Susannah Locke, Steven Belser, and Sarah Bishop Woods—and our Saturday crossword creators: Patrick Blindauer, Adesina O. Koiki, Will Nediger, and Andrew J. Ries. They bring their personality and style to their puzzles in a way I haven't seen in other venues (trust me, I do a lot of puzzles in other venues). I hope you enjoy solving these as much as I did.

Mom would be so proud.

—Elizabeth Crane
Vox puzzle editor

CLIMATE CHANGE AT THE MOVIES

BY PATRICK BLINDAUER

ACROSS

1 "Puttin' on the ___" ("Young Frankenstein" song)
5 Mia of soccer
9 Response to "Who's there?"
14 Spooky-sounding lake
15 Side times side, for a rectangle
16 Redd, Whitey, and Bluebeard, for example
17 2013 Disney film based on "The Snow Queen," after climate change
19 Step loudly, or clobber
20 Certain to get
21 White House nickname of the '50s
22 Urge to act
23 ___ Moines
24 Efron of "The Greatest Showman"
26 Challenge that may result in shaving cream all over someone's face
28 2003 Law/ Kidman/Zellweger war saga, after climate change
33 Rigel, for one
36 Garland on the poster for "Blue Hawaii"
37 Tempt successfully
38 Big name in skin care
40 Letterhead letters: Abbr.
42 Spud
43 Without an intermission, as a play
45 Thing pierced at a Claire's, perhaps
47 Fictional pooch with a repetitive name
48 1967 Paul Newman prison drama, after climate change
51 "Hey, ___" (way to get an iPhone to listen)
52 Forensic franchise
53 Weed whacker
56 Completely destroy, as my dad's 1967 Camaro (sorry, Dad)
59 Serengeti beast
61 Claims against property
63 Part of a moving experience, maybe
64 2013 romantic zombie comedy, after climate change
66 From then on
67 "Swan Lake" costume piece
68 Falco whose birthday is July 5, one day after mine
69 "Rescue Me" props
70 Unforeseen complication
71 Feels fluish, for example

DOWN

1 Gave a new look to
2 Ryan of "The Beverly Hillbillies"
3 Spats
4 "What did the ___ say to the 8?" "Nice belt!"
5 ___ to (must)
6 Preamble follower
7 Timid
8 Got by
9 "Ralph Breaks the ___"
10 Scheduling goal
11 Hazy atmospheric pollution
12 Company correspondence
13 Network to catch catchers
18 Minestrone pasta also known as risoni
25 Verizon acquisition of 2015
27 Vienna's country: Abbr.
28 Alfredo or béchamel, e.g.
29 Examined, as data
30 "Otto, You Ought to Take Me in Your ___" (1905 song)
31 "Law & Order: SVU" actor
32 Roman emperor after Claudius
33 Word before bank or blind
34 "Proud Mary" singer Turner
35 Solemnly swear
39 Greek warrior famous for his weak heel
41 Former capital city of India (as it was then known)
44 Road paving goo
46 Country with a red, white, and blue flag: Abbr.
49 "A Midsummer ___ Dream"
50 About 2.2 pounds, briefly
53 Schreck who wrote "What the Constitution Means to Me"
54 Buck of baseball
55 There are four in Mississippi
56 Fanny
57 Only U.S. state without a rectangular flag
58 Catches some rays
60 Person, place, or thing, for example
62 "What's the big ___?!"
65 Annoy

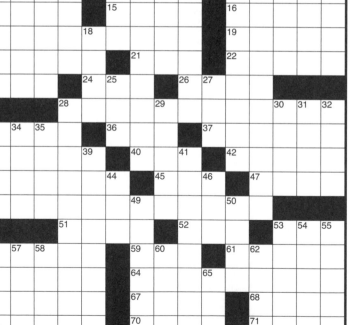

YOU'RE STARTING TO SCARE ME!

BY ADESINA O. KOIKI

ACROSS

1 Legislative body ordinance
4 Create, as trouble
10 Chandon's bubbly partner
14 Miracle-___
15 Accessory to abetting, perhaps?
16 "I think you're ___ something!"
17 Fair hiring letters
18 Legendary radio personality born Robert Weston Smith
20 Was no longer deceived by
22 Soft punch
23 Unfamiliar
24 NYC's Freedom Tower site: Abbr.
26 Equal level
29 Skin treatment
30 Former U.S. men's soccer captain Claudio
33 List of offerings
34 Katey Sagal's "Futurama" character
36 Some weightlifting movements
38 Wu-Tang Clan sobriquet
42 Surname of H.G. Wells's titular mad scientist
43 Bay Area superlative?
44 Leave out
45 Book cover info
47 Small margin of victory, idiomatically
51 "Didn't I tell you?"
52 Layer of farmland?
53 Halloween beverage
54 Persistently pester
56 Having an identity matching one's sex assignment at birth
60 "Oo ee, oo aa aa, ting, tang, walla walla bing bang" utterer of song
63 Jersey sound
64 At any point in time
65 2001 French film that earned five Oscar nominations
66 One half of a landmark 1970 merger: Abbr.
67 Miami-___ County
68 Wading birds related to egrets
69 66-Across's merger partner: Abbr.

DOWN

1 May-December relationship discrepancy
2 Zydeco inventors, ethnically
3 "The Facts of Life" role
4 Greeted cordially at the door
5 Uncles, in Spanish
6 What teams are during a bye
7 Diplomatic falling-out
8 Not cut, as a lawn
9 Group for good drivers?: Abbr.
10 Austin Powers's "superpower"
11 How some court cases are won
12 List-ending abbreviation
13 Tik___
19 "Superstore" network
21 Firmly established
25 Doggedly deal with
27 Actress Kendrick
28 Famed Canadian rock band
30 Flatly deny
31 Widely taught American school subject: Abbr.
32 Luxurious boat
33 Brown skin pigment
35 LAX information
37 Descriptor for Wayne and Nas X
38 DNA-altered biotech products: Abbr.
39 E.T.'s quest
40 Set straight
41 Choice sushi tidbit
46 It's reported to the IRS
48 Person who is always out?
49 Escort away
50 ___ Garner, composer of the jazz standard "Misty"
52 Pituitary gland substance that is also created synthetically: Abbr.
53 Roman goddess of agriculture
55 One of Yellowstone's 2.2 million
57 Birthday cake detailer, often
58 Normandy battle site of WWII
59 "I'm ___ Down" (1995 Mary J. Blige hit)
60 "With this ring I thee ___ ..."
61 1997 French Open champ Majoli
62 "Zip-a-Dee-Doo-___"

SYNCED UP

BY WILL NEDIGER

ACROSS

1 Toledo's country
6 Something you might subscribe to online
10 Canine that looks like a mop
14 ___ Pocket (Mattel line)
15 About, on a memo
16 Mineral mined in Australia
17 *Anticipated eagerly*
20 "Mein Gott!"
21 2006 film set in Georgia's capital
22 Cozy reading spots
23 *Comment about karma*
28 Bled in the wash
29 Group in a coop
30 Picked hairdos
33 "Life on ___" (Tracy K. Smith poetry collection)
35 Spider's creation
38 *Cult classic starring Meryl Streep and Goldie Hawn*
42 Do some darning
43 Freshly
44 Canadian civil rights activist Desmond

45 Attitude
47 March sister played by Emma Watson
48 *Grooming expert on "Queer Eye"*
56 Marinade in Latin American cuisine
57 Hard to walk on without slipping, perhaps
58 Wager
59 Barbershop quartet feature ... or what you get when you string together the last words of the answers to the italicized clues?
64 Join together
65 Alternative clothing item to a salwar kameez

66 Cropped up
67 Greek god of war
68 Seoul music?
69 "Sounds awful!"

DOWN

1 Food fight sound
2 Pupper
3 It means "hello" and "goodbye"
4 Variety
5 "Science Guy" Bill
6 Amendment you might "plead"
7 "___ Holmes" (2020 Netflix film)
8 Screw up
9 Drops on the grass
10 Not watertight
11 "What's ___?" (response in a classic prank)

12 Hanukkah pancake
13 Dejected comment after a game
18 Crowing time
19 Unknown author, briefly
24 Easy gait
25 Over-the-shoulder band
26 Try to make fetch happen?
27 Quaint assent
30 Some extensions block them
31 ATM charge
32 Like the fish in a poke bowl
33 High-IQ society since 1946
34 Not experiencing physical attraction, briefly

35 "That name doesn't ring a bell"
36 Slithery swimmer
37 Nursing purchase
39 Talk trash about
40 Like all leap years
41 Endorse in ink
45 Buffalo NHL team
46 Perched upon
47 People in both ancient and modern Mesoamerica
48 ___ cake (British treat)
49 Stench, in Canada
50 Futile
51 The "N" in TNT
52 Technology whose first letter stands for "violence"
53 Kindle download
54 Touch or taste
55 Ocular afflictions
60 "___ me anything"
61 Genre for MC Lyte
62 Line in a kid's drawing of the Sun
63 Test in a tube

CAN I GET A WORD IN?

BY ANDREW J. RIES

ACROSS

1 Sulk
5 Gives the green light to
8 Disapproval, in slang
13 Catholic hymn sung at weddings and funerals
15 Training groups
17 *Headline on the April 1997 cover of Time featuring Ellen DeGeneres*
18 Confidently declare
19 Colgate competitor
20 ___'easter (New England storm)
22 The "S" in the pop supergroup LSD
23 *Item worn by the leader of the Tour de France*
28 When repeated, avid
31 Brazilian metropolis, for short
32 Adores
33 "Unfortunately ..."
35 His catchphrase is "I pity the fool"
37 Loathe
40 *Distinctly American trait of problem-solving ability*
44 Pull the plug on a relationship
45 Pennsylvania governor Wolf succeeded by Josh Shapiro
46 "___: Legacy" (2010 sci-fi sequel)
47 Free of frills
50 Unlikely election result
52 Driver's peg
53 *"That's not a good idea"*
57 Noise booster at a concert
58 Debt note
59 2019 NFL MVP Lamar Jackson, for one
63 Musicians mentioned in "The Twelve Days of Christmas"
66 One way to get a word in ... and an aural hint to a feature of the italicized clues' answers
69 Wonder with 25 Grammys
70 Moniker prior to a gender transition
71 Staircase series
72 Tidal recession
73 Conveyance on a snowy hill

DOWN

1 BLT condiment
2 Exceeding
3 Salt-N-___ (classic rap group)
4 Deschanel of "Bones"
5 Common web address ending
6 Maker of the Sorento SUV
7 Refuse
8 "Marriage Story" co-star, in headlines
9 "Rumor ___ it ..."
10 Features of free apps, often
11 Formal button-up item, maybe
12 Spine-tingling
14 Orangish color
16 Command to a dog
21 Hooting bird
24 Vodka tonic garnish
25 "Shark Tank" investor Greiner
26 "Dear ___ Hansen" (Tony-winning musical)
27 Give an opposing argument
28 Country musician Collin
29 British comic Carr
30 Character fashioned from a glove
34 Aptitude
36 Explosive stuff, for short
38 Oklahoma tribe
39 Baseball Hall of Famer Sandberg
41 "And others," in citations
42 Usual order, informally
43 Ruler in a Muslim nation
48 Shorebirds with long bills
49 Opposite of paleo-
51 Slipped up
53 Talks, talks, talks
54 Leaves out
55 Leather with a rough finish
56 Shows boredom, in a way
60 Chemist's small bottle
61 "Twilight" vampire
62 Require
64 Night before
65 Strongly criticize
67 Haaland serving as Secretary of the Interior
68 Chatterbox's "gift"

LUPITA SAYS

BY PATRICK BLINDAUER

ACROSS

1 Says "bye" to, in Bordeaux
10 It merged with Mobil
15 Regional IDs
16 Fix, as a loose lace
17 With 36-Across and 61-Across, a quote by Lupita Nyong'o
18 Singer who released "21" in '11
19 Harp, for one
20 Monopoly board quartet: Abbr.
22 Get ___ of (toss out)
23 Places for skates and kites, perhaps
26 Warhol muse Sedgwick
28 Designer of St. Paul's Cathedral in London
29 "___ Believer" (1966 hit)
30 "Turn! Turn! Turn!" band, with "the"
31 Arthur's nickname in "The Once and Future King"
32 Casino area
33 Surname of baseball brothers
34 "Didn't need to hear that!"
36 See 17-Across
41 Texter's "incidentally"
42 "Show Boat" composer Jerome
43 Son of Noah
45 Longtime Vicki Lawrence role
48 Choose democratically
50 Code-breaking org.
51 Skincare brand that sounds like it might be Spanish
52 Military status
53 "The War of the Worlds" radio broadcast, unintentionally
54 Breast Cancer Awareness Mo.
55 Clicking sound
56 Tribe known for its kachina dolls
59 Chuck who co-created "The Big Bang Theory"
61 See 17-Across
66 For the birds?
67 Deli counter selection
68 Put a whammy on
69 Constellation near Cassiopeia

DOWN

1 ___ Ems (German spa town)
2 Sales item abbr.
3 Country singer Jo ___ Messina
4 Cars that sound mournful
5 Zenith
6 Booster, for example
7 Phrase before many a foolish act
8 Musket attachment?
9 Handle, say
10 Time pieces
11 Put two lines through
12 SUV retired in 2015
13 More viscous
14 Negative contraction
21 Begin again
23 Word before code or file
24 Leave out
25 Swear words?
27 Like a certain sailor of song
28 Subj. of the board game Memoir '44
30 Devices for leaves or snow, but not at the same time
33 Not fore
35 Craig of the Rockies, for one: Abbr.
37 Site that sounds like Pig Latin for a common verb
38 One who does some swabbing
39 "Drat! Foiled again!"
40 Org. that works with SpaceX
44 "Where the Wild Things Are" kid
45 Cabbage or clams
46 Recess
47 Mathematical array
49 Great Plains tribe
53 Good name for somebody in HR
55 Take care of, with "to"
57 Ilhan in the House
58 Mexican bread
60 Alec Baldwin's middle name
62 "We Are Young" band
63 Spot of land in la mer
64 Rude dude
65 Lovelace who wrote the first computer program

TOUCHDOWN DANCE

BY ADESINA O. KOIKI

ACROSS

1 Impasse
7 Rainbow mnemonic first name
10 Rum ___ Tugger ("Cats" role)
13 Recovering, say
15 Harvey Dent's nom de crime
17 *Start of a round*
18 *Like a flame from a Bunsen burner with an uncovered airhole*
19 Caroline du Nord, par exemple
20 Org. with a scholarly publishing handbook
22 Make up (for)
23 NBA reporter Gold-Onwude
24 *Word liable to be misinterpreted if said to a non-native*
27 "The ___ that men do ..."
29 Ruined one's mascara, perhaps
30 Borders
32 Muslim festival
33 Fond du ___, Wisconsin
36 *Alabama Slammer ingredient*
41 Bernard Shaw's former station
42 Goat's young
43 Light weight
44 St. Peter's Basilica attraction
46 Carol or aria
47 *Having made it through a hairy situation in one piece*
51 Private sch. located in Dallas
54 Advancing weather system
55 Something past due?
56 Cooking instruction
57 *Feature used in file transfers among Apple devices*
60 Area that sees lots of spikes, in a way ... and a feature in each of the answers to the six italicized clues

DOWN

62 Free time
63 Cancún's peninsula
64 Inc. relative
65 Babe Ruth's was 0.87 in World Series play
66 Analyzed very closely

DOWN

1 1,000 cubic centimeters
2 "You're ___ talk!"
3 Auto mechanic's lubricator
4 Blackhearts frontwoman
5 Hawaiian seafood option
6 Bat, for one
7 Instant, automated process of buying ads online; Abbr.
8 Tootsie Pop licker (and eater) in a famous ad
9 1983 Lionel Richie hit
10 Chevrolet SUV
11 Women's b-ball powerhouse
12 Dealt (out)
14 Students and boxers may get saved by it
16 Malodorous
21 Rising in influence
24 Plenty of ___ (dating app)
25 Calif. congressman Swalwell
26 Abe Lincoln's dog
28 Nov. 11 honoree
30 Get-out-of-PC-jail key
31 Lemon formerly of 41-Across
33 Hopes against all hope
34 Jeanne d'___
35 Brain condition closely associated with contact sports: Abbr.
37 Just got (by)
38 EGOT attainer Moreno
39 Invader of Iberia during the 8th century
40 Merriment
44 Abodes for toads
45 "Assuming that's correct ..."
46 Escorted to the top floor, say
47 Words after first or most
48 "Paradise Lost" archangel
49 Doughnut-shaped
50 London sky colour, most days
52 Singer/actress Janelle
53 Overturn
56 Government policy head
58 The Bruins' legendary #4
59 Sleep disrupter in a Hans Christian Andersen fairy tale
61 Beltway hub: Abbr.

IT'S ALL RELATIVE

BY WILL NEDIGER

ACROSS

1 Dye holders
5 Possessed
8 Peninsula once called al-Andalus
14 "It's my time to shine!"
15 "Tokyo Story" director Yasujiro ___
16 Lebanese trees
17 Perfect match
19 Civil rights activist Cummings
20 Org. that helps enforce the ACA
21 Fired
22 Fraction of a byte
23 Entertainment on the trip to Canterbury
25 Haida vehicle
27 Bungler
30 Gumshoe
32 Tactic that might involve a shelter
34 "___ Madness" (anti-cannabis movie)
36 Part of speech of the answer to this clue
37 "Personally ..."
40 Like some receptions
43 Do a follow-up job after sowing
44 Grocery store pathways
46 Remiss
49 Descriptor for Spenser's "Queene"
53 "Let me think ..."
54 Winning
56 Language whose edition of Wikipedia was discovered in 2020 to have about 33% of its articles written by a contributor who wasn't fluent in that language
57 "Sweet Dreams (___ Made of This)"
58 NPR Shop purchase
60 Venomous snake
61 With 64-Across, Audre Lorde book ... or a hint to this puzzle's shaded letters
64 See 61-Across
66 Waiting at a stoplight
67 Be too curious
68 Reinhart of "Riverdale" and "Hustlers"
69 Repetitive nickname for singer Swift
70 Class that teaches SVO word order
71 Tinder swipe direction

DOWN

1 Drops in on
2 Indifferent to ethics
3 Dishevel, as hair
4 Show announced by Darrell Hammond, briefly
5 Elaborate deception
6 Tenochtitlan resident
7 Labor day, maybe?
8 Place where you might save your plums for breakfast
9 Showed to be false
10 Fix a typo, e.g.
11 British rule in India
12 George Gershwin's lyricist brother
13 Mount Vesuvius substance
18 Learn absolutely perfectly
24 Home of Albania and Austria
26 Rats out, with "on"
27 Something "eaten" by a shoe insert
28 Feverish fit
29 Ward (off)
31 Clothing line
33 "Hold that thought"
35 Huge spread
37 Eyebrow shape
38 Clothing line
39 Kibbutz, often
41 Sitcom alien who's "back ... in Pog form!" on an episode of "The Simpsons"
42 Flirts with, maybe
45 Carbon-13 or plutonium-238
47 Hickok who had a relationship with Eleanor Roosevelt
48 Vitality
50 Tour employee
51 "The investment pays for ___!"
52 Quickness of wit
55 Does some barista work
57 Squabbling
59 "Until next time," in a text
61 "Make yourself comfortable!"
62 Investigative journalist ___ B. Wells
63 Foxlike
65 Not feeling 100%

PRESENT COMPANY INCLUDED

BY ANDREW J. RIES

ACROSS

1 Quarrel
5 One of the corners on a Monopoly board
9 Play groups
14 Like the driven snow, so it's said
15 Unit of farmland
16 Brown who hosts "Good Eats"
17 ___ mater
18 Buses often run on it
20 Jai Alai from Cigar City Brewing, e.g.
21 Gave a meal to
22 Cobb or caprese, perhaps
23 Japanese assassin of old
25 Prefix for space and dynamic
26 Close kin, informally
29 Continental southernmost point that translates to "land of fire"
33 Off-the-wall
34 Releases
35 "I Love Me" singer Lovato
38 Purplish vegetables
41 Part of an underling's title: Abbr.
42 People who follow a set of rules called the Ordnung
44 Attracted (to)

46 French philosopher who wrote "Madness and Civilization"
51 To the ___ degree
52 Reddish-white horse
53 Acronym describing aspirin or ibuprofen
55 Hayes in the Rock and Roll Hall of Fame
57 Auction action
59 Tribe after whom a western U.S. state is named
60 Venezuelan attraction whose main plunge measures over 2,600 feet
63 Important stretches of years
64 Many hipster bros have one

65 Very insightful
66 Connection
67 Ice cream parlor supply
68 Circular current in a river
69 Come clean, with "up"

DOWN

1 Its capital is Madrid
2 Preacher's speaking spot
3 Major Italian fashion house
4 The world's second most consumed beverage, after water
5 Green gemstone
6 Battery fluid
7 Blind rage
8 Apartment dweller, perhaps

9 Cancel
10 ___ Romeo (sports car manufacturer)
11 Payments made by horse breeders
12 Digit on a foot
13 Show with three "At Home" episodes in 2020, for short
19 Tupper who invented Tupperware
21 Cabbie's customer
24 Like Hanukkah celebrants
25 Attached, as a new wing of a building
27 Gets older
28 Highest in number
30 Part of a cage of bones

31 "Come as You ___" (Nirvana song)
32 Planet classified as an ice giant
35 Exclamation sometimes preceded by "hot"
36 Radiate
37 State comprised of two peninsulas
39 ___ TV (channel with much reality programming)
40 Cul-de-___
43 Introduces with great fanfare
45 Stick at a magic show
47 Bakery purchase
48 Superficial appearance
49 Metcalf of "Lady Bird"
50 NFL team that calls Nashville home
54 Classroom stations
56 Very dry
57 Oozed (out)
58 Children's book series for finding objects in photos
60 Easy as ___
61 "The Matrix" protagonist
62 Directed
63 Christmas figure seen in the answers to 18-, 29-, 46-, and 60-Across

13

YULE BE HEARING FROM ME

BY PATRICK BLINDAUER

ACROSS

1 ___-mo
4 1982 teen comedy
10 They may be caught
14 ___ culpa
15 Predatory lender
16 Paul who sang "Put Your Head on My Shoulder"
17 Kin of a Roman poet?
20 Liable to cause nightmares
21 Certain physical reaction catalyst
22 Show quickly, as a badge
25 "The Lion King" baddie
27 40 or 44, in STL, e.g.
28 "Alias" org.
29 "Life ___ Highway" (Rascal Flatts cover)
32 Comment made directly to the crowd
34 Lincoln follower: Abbr.
35 Stocking stuff
37 One of many sworn to Sauron
39 Civilization that's obsessed with certain pigeons?
43 Running back ___ Benjamin of the New Orleans Saints

44 What fresh mulch and not-so-fresh meat make, for example
45 Place to crash for the night
47 "Help!" actor
50 Bring down to the station
51 Hamm of soccer fame
52 "Much ___ About Nothing"
54 Looked for damages
56 President-___
58 Has, in a way
60 Childish retort
63 John Hancocks on giant checks?
68 Chief Norse god
69 "Got me"
70 "All Those Years ___" (George Harrison song)

71 Check for quarters?
72 Quakers in the Rockies
73 Sounds from Santa (and what's been added to 17-, 39-, and 63-Across)

DOWN

1 "I can't believe it," in a text
2 MGM mascot's name
3 "Life of Pi" prop
4 Ratatouille ingredient
5 Not ashore
6 Sound of contentment
7 Emulates a hungry lion
8 Anago, at a Japanese restaurant
9 "Wit" and "Doubt," for two
10 "A Little Fall of ___" ("Les Misérables" song)
11 "Let's do it later on"
12 "Amirite?"
13 Fresh, in a way
18 Jerk
19 "Burnt Toast" author Hatcher
22 TV monitoring gp.
23 Slender and graceful
24 "A Few Good Men" playwright
26 Whitewater rafting locale
30 Thesaurus offering: Abbr.
31 Harvard roommate of Tommy Lee Jones
33 Uno + uno

36 Off
38 Pessimistic person
40 Bon ___ (clever comment)
41 Org. that agreed in 2020 to a $2.5 million fine to settle New York charges
42 Carcinogenic fireproofing material
46 Washington ballplayer, briefly
48 Far from flushed in the face
49 Where rubles are spent
52 Detest
53 Semiconductor with two terminals
55 Find, as facts
57 Football Hall of Famer Groza
59 Home on the range, say
61 Queen of England from 1702 to 1714
62 "Magnolia" soundtrack singer Aimee
64 What a bouncer checks
65 Word of good cheer?
66 "Ratatouille" food critic Anton
67 "Mayday!"

RING IN THE NEW YEAR

BY ADESINA O. KOIKI

ACROSS

1 Decorate a cake
4 He/they made an NBA debut in 1979/1989
9 Skilled trade
14 More: Spanish
15 Main character in "The Honeymooners"
16 The "R" in NPR
17 Plant with edible shoots that's related to lilies
19 Performance with arias
20 Foolish person
21 Popular initialism framing one's emotions about a specific moment
23 Fortune-telling prop
27 "That's obvious!"
30 ___-turvy
31 Cheez Doodles food company
32 Council site of the 1500s
34 Three-leafed find ... unless one gets lucky, of course
36 Talking blues musician known for his iconic 1962 hit "Boom Boom"
39 Dick ___, Pro Football Hall of Famer who popularized the zone blitz defense
40 Lorna ___
41 Appear to be
42 Out of bounds, say
44 Like over 30 of Arkansas's counties
45 Opposite
50 21st Greek letter
51 Ran on 16-Across
53 Request from a person wanting a high five
57 December 26, in some parts of the world ... or an apt title for this puzzle given the "gifts" contained inside four answers
61 June birthstone
62 Unreactive, as a gas
63 Summer, in Marseille
64 Saw logs at night
65 45's better half, often
66 Blog feed initials

DOWN

1 Mononymous Somali supermodel
2 G-Shock watch maker
3 Cable channel for college sports
4 "Real Love" singer ___ Blige
5 In the style of
6 Entertainer's engagement
7 Restricted hospital area: Abbr.
8 Jai alai equipment
9 Bunch of spectators
10 Style for certain music battles
11 King Sunny ___ (Afro-pop pioneer)
12 Cone-bearing evergreen tree
13 Trigonometrical counterpart to SOH and CAH
18 Boyhood nickname in "The Phantom Menace"
22 SpongeBob and, previously, Jim, at the Krusty Krab
24 Noshed at noon, say
25 Something picked during a disagreement
26 Decided one would
27 Embellish one's fall, in soccer
28 Person logging in
29 Five-time Grammy winner whose pseudonym stands for "_aving _verything _evealed"
31 Socially conscious
32 Us vs. ___
33 Protein synthesis molecule
35 Horror heavyweight Chaney
36 Yell insults
37 Be a flunky to
38 Univ. of Virginia athletes, to their fans (they're not the Owls, trust me on this!)
39 '60s psychedelic
43 Small African antelopes
45 "Criminal" singer (1997)
46 Coca-Cola's fruit-flavored cousin
47 18-wheeler
48 Primates, for humans
49 Vegetarians' taboos
52 Uses Clairol, perhaps
53 FedEx rival
54 Enclosure
55 Chinese "way"
56 Bobby of Boston Bruins fame
58 Demon of Japanese folklore
59 ___ out (deleted, in a way)
60 Choleric state

15

MIDDLE GROUND

BY WILL NEDIGER

ACROSS

1 Guitarist's time to shine
5 Bowie's rock genre
9 A whole bunch
14 Eats
15 Result of a big fight
16 Hair-raising
17 Dish cooked in broth
19 Addressee of many voice commands
20 Requests from
21 Numbing pattern
23 Supervillain's hangout
24 Bite-sized
25 4G ___
27 Easy run
29 Partner of "parks"
30 "Don't be a stranger"
34 Soccer star Lloyd
35 Debate
36 ___-chic
39 Harmonizes
42 Nile biters

43 Avoid worrying about the guest list
45 Company with an orange-and-white fleet
47 Lay off
53 "Killing ___"
54 Laverne of "Orange Is the New Black"
55 K–12 org.
56 You, but not you specifically
57 Company that now makes the Super Soaker
59 Speaker in a car
61 Cheese that's often grated
63 Decorative fabric
65 Point hit hard by an earthquake ... or what's found in this puzzle's theme answers

67 ___ notes (album info)
68 "The ___-Motion" (Little Eva hit)
69 Latte option
70 "Pomp and Circumstance" composer
71 Stagger
72 Goddess often cheated on by Zeus

DOWN

1 Unreadable writing
2 "Gotcha"
3 Treasured possession, often
4 Has creditors
5 Con artists
6 Adjective before Pump or Peep

7 From quite a distance
8 Peak often depicted by Hokusai
9 Salt source
10 Home alternative
11 Some room accents
12 Water cooler item
13 Browsing history features
18 Wisconsin's official state dance
22 Whole bunch
26 Slippery
28 Region that includes Canada's biggest city, briefly
31 Extent
32 Prison wall poster, stereotypically

33 Grad students' stressors
36 "Go easy on me!"
37 Mediterranean staple
38 Acting like a helicopter parent
40 Double-dipper's germ transmitter
41 Annual pub crawl near Christmas
44 End-of-list abbr.
46 Tsar's proclamation
48 Refuse to share
49 De-class-ifies?
50 Utterly despise
51 Not idling
52 Illinois city that represents Middle America
58 Insect in a John Donne poem
60 Catch a glimpse of
62 Rainfall unit
64 Mess up
66 Hosp. zone

OFF TO A ROARING START

BY ANDREW J. RIES

ACROSS

1 Morning ringer
6 Acronym for the best ever
10 Source of much celebrity news
13 Home of mandopop
14 High-fiber fruit
15 Tough row to ___
16 The ground in Zimbabwe's capital city?
18 Critical hospital section: Abbr.
19 Direction opposite WNW
20 Trade
21 General, captain, lieutenant, etc.
23 Pop alternative
24 Felt disdain for a certain radio format?
27 Breeze producer
28 Sci-fi novelist Cline
30 Pat and Vanna's show, for short
33 Heckler's utterance
35 Heckler's utterance
37 Emphatic answer to "Who's the best musician named Isaac?"
41 "Bravo!"
42 Remove, as from power
43 Animal depicted on Mexico's flag
44 Streep's three
47 Rower's propeller
48 Element of a nun's uniform?
51 Prompt to an attack dog
54 Cylindrical deli offerings
56 ___ League (22-country coalition)
57 "The War with Grandpa" co-star Thurman
58 Provide help to
59 Nincompoop ... or a feature of this puzzle's theme answers?
63 Wedding vow response
64 Some attendees at a family gathering
65 Ski resort dwelling
66 Far from ample
67 Pursuits for enterprising students?: Abbr.
68 Bird call

DOWN

1 Throbbed with pain
2 Tibet's largest city
3 Broadcasted
4 Messenger ___ (genetic material)
5 Fire safety inspectors
6 Purple soda flavor
7 My and your
8 Insect with "fire" and "carpenter" species
9 Locale of Imam Khomeini Airport
10 Sets lofty goals, say
11 Make fun of
12 Mount Olympus ruler
14 Distinct aroma of Islay Scotch
17 McGregor of "Doctor Sleep"
22 Top-fermented beer
25 Initial public offering
26 Arbor Day planting
27 Service charge
29 Maynard James Keenan's Grammy-winning band
30 "Am I supposed to know this person?"
31 Ring over an angel
32 Cosmetic product applied under a brow
33 Compete in a Renaissance Faire event
34 Measures of academic acuity: Abbr.
36 ___-hit wonder
38 Seaweed at a sushi bar
39 Driver's restraint
40 Supply for a road crew
45 High limit
46 FBI sting depicted in "American Hustle"
47 Mouth-related
49 Agreements
50 Large boats
51 Leather with a fuzzy texture
52 Certain Google search result
53 Service academy student
54 Stray animal
55 Tilt-A-Whirl, for one
60 Central point
61 "A" in Spanish
62 "___ do you sleep at night?"

"SEE YOU LATER, ALLIGATOR!"

BY PATRICK BLINDAUER

ACROSS

1 Go over again
7 No. on a college transcript
10 Start to board?
14 Singer at Barack's first inauguration
15 It comes after Doris Day in "We Didn't Start the Fire"
17 Chomp at
18 Big name in auto racing
19 With 20-Across, "The Sound of Music" song
20 See 19-Across
21 Quantity of sheets
23 "Judge not, ___ ye be judged"
24 Plays for a fool
27 How vegetables can be eaten
29 They may be weathered
33 Engaged
34 Phishing expeditions
36 Currency of China
37 With 38- and 39-Across, *NSYNC hit of 2000
38 See 37-Across
39 See 37-Across
40 Freshly
42 Pays dollars for quarters?
44 Cutting comment
45 Have a little something
46 Threw back a fish, say
47 More diluted
49 Feature of the St. Louis skyline
51 Necklaces that sound like a potato chip company
52 With 55-Across, 1961 hit for Ray Charles
55 See 52-Across
59 Emblematic
60 Sees eye to eye about
61 Setting for "Romeo and Juliet"
62 It remains unpopped during a wheelie
63 People person?
64 Ballpark figure: Abbr.
65 All there, in a way

DOWN

1 Scott Joplin tunes
2 With 30-Down, inventor of a twistable toy
3 Respond to a doctor's efforts
4 If everything else fails
5 Did the light thing?
6 Buildings on some bases
7 Tennis champion Steffi
8 "Young lady, are you familiar with the ___ codes in this state?": "Kentucky Fried Movie"
9 17325 is part of Gettysburg's
10 Boxer's plaything
11 Lo-cal, in ads
12 ___ Phonetic Alphabet: Abbr.
13 Bucket
16 Design on a feudal coat
22 "The Scottish Play"
24 Keith of country
25 Deliver a veto
26 Fencing tools that do not appear in "Fences"
28 Manor where Alfred buttles
30 See 2-Down
31 "Perhaps"
32 Evil grin
35 "Have we ___?"
41 So on
42 Pit sight that reads the same forward and backward
43 Cuss out
44 Range features, perhaps
48 Stuffing for quilts
50 ___ Hero (balancing card game)
51 Prime theater sections
52 Abode for certain buzzers
53 Like some tea
54 Amos whose "Little Earthquakes" I probably listened to 1,000 times growing up
55 Hard to come by
56 ___ Cup (cricket tournament since 1983)
57 Ear pieces?
58 Joint for banjo players

ALUMINUM-INATING

BY ADESINA O. KOIKI

ACROSS

1 Venomous African snake
6 Sand castle need
10 "I'm rubber, you're ___ ..."
14 Expanse of ice
15 Contributes (to)
16 1996 Tony Award winner for Best Musical
17 It's drawn in every head-to-head sports matchup ... unless the game ends in a 0–0 tie
19 Respectively
20 Available, at a bar
21 Bracelet location, perhaps
22 Mike's partner in the candy section
25 Crust, to the Earth
28 Answer a stimulus
31 South African grassland
32 It spoils a perfect game, but not a no-hitter
33 Term of endearment
36 Behind-the-scenes activity
39 Pago Pago people
40 "Boy ___ World" ('90s ABC sitcom)
42 Runaway victory
43 Optional section of the SAT
44 Desperate measure
50 Uncertain, on a schedule: Abbr.
51 Diarist Nin
52 Controlling power
55 Sets of equipment
56 Technique used to multiply $(x + 4)(x - 5)$, with the first words of 17-, 25-, 36-, and 44-Across making up its mnemonic
61 Give off, as radiation
62 Founder's inspiration
63 "Lovergirl" singer ___ Marie
64 Part of 1-Down
65 Have faith in, with "on"
66 Apply some perfume, perhaps

DOWN

1 Humanitarian organization translated to English as "Doctors Without Borders": Abbr.
2 Tuna variety
3 Debussy's "La ___"
4 Kiss, en español
5 Office memo heading: Abbr.
6 Pacific Ocean island republic east of the Philippines
7 Fail at fostering a rescue, in a sense
8 Merger announcement?
9 Psychedelic championed by Timothy Leary
10 St. Vincent and the ___
11 Like some faucets or roofs
12 "I give up!"
13 2001 Nas song that has become a standard for hip-hop diss tracks
18 "Takin' Care of Business" band, for short
21 Ever
22 Lividity
23 "The Americans" actress Russell
24 Brings in
26 Civil rights activist Medgar
27 Stink horribly
29 They make a racket
30 Small earthquakes
33 Quid pro quo transactions
34 Triumphed
35 Cast out of the body
37 The Eternal City
38 Sudden sharp pain
41 Name of a 2000 Summer Olympics official mascot (the one that was a platypus, in case you were wondering)
44 "Great" components
45 Jungian inner personality
46 Smooth material
47 Variety of window typically supported by corbels
48 Track race involving batons
49 ___ Hortons
53 NBA team that calls Barclays Center home
54 Single part of a process
56 Evergreen tree variety
57 Emotive poem
58 Pronoun for ladies
59 Words before dare or whim
60 Night's opposite

OFF TO A GOOD START

BY WILL NEDIGER

ACROSS

1 "A Suitable Boy" channel
4 Source for financial news
8 Guinea-___ (Guinea neighbor)
14 Miriam Makeba hairstyle, casually
15 "There is no Dana, only ___": "Ghostbusters"
16 Pair taken for a headache, perhaps
17 *Fandango?*
19 Faculty hangout
20 "Symphonies of Wind Instruments" composer Stravinsky
21 Meal for a baleen whale
23 "Who Framed Roger Rabbit" frame
24 Zeal
25 Murder mystery suspect, often
26 High point of a building
28 Patrisse Cullors's movement, briefly
29 *Toyota?*
31 "That's correct"
32 Places with a lot of buzz?
34 Dresses often worn with niqabs
36 "Words, Words, Words" playwright David
37 "Seriously???"
38 Region
41 Like Christmas presents, often
45 Allah created him from clay
46 *Sealyham terrier?*
48 Minecraft material
49 Silences on Zoom
51 Got 100% on
52 Shore projection
53 "You clumsy ___!"
54 "Kiss the chef" garment
56 Bunch of actors
57 Dragstrip sounds
59 *Badminton?*
62 Really handsome man
63 "You can say that again"
64 Prefix with liberal
65 Jerry, but not Tom
66 Depend
67 Space between incisors, for some

DOWN

1 Person you DM every day, maybe
2 System with embossed dots
3 *Connect Four?*
4 Official who's in charge
5 Monastic in Buddhism or Christianity
6 Horse chestnuts
7 White-collar workers?
8 Really fun time
9 Adored celebrities
10 Mariska Hargitay's show, for short
11 *Singapore?*
12 Mostly Arab-Berber country
13 No help at all
18 Dress up in, as gay apparel
22 Financial adviser's suggestion, maybe: Abbr.
24 ___ and flow
25 Gets ready to click
27 Martha Argerich's instrument
29 Record to watch later, in a way
30 Strict disciplinarian
33 "I'll take another card"
35 "Parasite" director Joon-ho
37 Agent's alias
38 Russian tea holder
39 Facebook co-founder Saverin
40 *Catsup?*
41 Buffet with guacamole
42 *"Popcorn"?*
43 Country in the Horn of Africa
44 "Nothing but ___!"
47 Musician's asset
50 "Salt, Fat, Acid, Heat" author Nosrat
52 Sucker
55 Note-passer's sound
56 "Ohio" band, for short
58 Number of Z's in this puzzle grid
60 Lana ___ Rey
61 Blouse or cami

SWITCH POSITIONS

by Andrew J. Ries

ACROSS

1 "My thoughts exactly!"
5 "Tenet" genre, for short
10 "___ Don't Lie" (Shakira hit)
14 Fuzzy glow
15 Recorded, in a way
16 Berry that resembles a grape
17 Storm, Beast, and others
18 Native of an Arabian Peninsula country
19 Minnesota's WNBA team
20 He became the U.S. Senate's youngest current member when he was sworn in at age 33 on January 20, 2021
23 Narrow channel
26 Tiny metric unit of length
30 Find a new purpose for
31 Con's opposite
34 Michael of "Tenet"
35 Stimulating midday mugful
38 Casual top
39 Sleep ___
40 Short-lived obsession
41 Task to be "run"
44 Far from hefty
47 Target for hammering
49 Convince
50 Something mulled over by a free agent
55 In the style of
56 One of the Five W's
57 Truck stop sight
59 Y-shaped football formation
66 Burdensome
67 Allowance for a traveling employee
68 Property manager
69 Blues great Muddy

DOWN

1 Line on a receipt
2 Make sounds with a closed mouth
3 Anger
4 Self-professed "capital of Silicon Valley"
5 Rolling ___
6 Hunter's garb, for short
7 Makeup of a hoppy flight: Abbr.
8 Swampy lands
9 Non-literal expression
10 Rhyming descriptor of some beans
11 Like some winter roads
12 Go for the gold?
13 Pack quantity, maybe
21 Wrapped up
22 ___ score (credit risk rating)
23 Sewer cover
24 Point (to)
25 Exterior
27 Participates in improv
28 "Inside the NBA" analyst
29 Attention-starved
31 Firecracker sound
32 NFL coach Rivera
33 Formula ___
36 Bottommost point
37 Often-uncredited appearance
42 Novelist Patchett
43 "Paper Towns" star Wolff
45 One of Santa's helpers
46 '80s sitcom featuring the Tanner family
48 Suburban growths
49 Bend over
50 "So Wrong" singer Patsy
51 Places of refuge
52 "Weekend Update" co-anchor with Jost
53 Bert's bud
54 Platform for a choir singer
55 Nowhere to be seen
58 Precious rocks
60 Softball slams: Abbr.
61 "You stink!"
62 "Days of ___ Lives"
63 Small amount
64 Title for a monk
65 Summertime clock standard in NYC

"ALL YOU NEED IS LOVE"

BY PATRICK BLINDAUER

ACROSS

1 F-___
5 Unappetizing chow
9 Old Russian monarch
13 Willie who was the first black player in the NHL
14 Raise, as children
15 Basketball infractions
16 Princess who wields a chakram
17 Start to freeze?
18 Planetary path
19 Hit song for the Supremes and Phil Collins
22 "There is a wind that never dies": Yoko ___
23 Tony-nominated Phillipa of "Hamilton"
24 Near-the-belt bulges
29 Squirting squid organ
34 Michael and Sarah's director on "The Phantom of the Opera"
35 Clef whose middle line is C
37 Ma's forte
38 Keats or Coleridge
41 "All systems go"
42 Kindle purchase
43 Word before nonsense or chaos
44 Screenwriter/director Ephron
46 Curly colleague
47 Roto-___
49 Job that's not a chore
52 Point of no return?
54 Scand. country
55 "Frozen" song that ends with a proposal
62 "___ be expected ..."
64 "I couldn't agree more!"
65 The ___ of Cats (board game)
66 Do some grieving
67 Trig follower, perhaps
68 Rickman who won a 69-Across for "Rasputin: Dark Servant of Destiny"
69 Award won by 68-Across Rickman for "Rasputin: Dark Servant of Destiny" (is there an echo in here?)
70 Place for a tiny house
71 Barn area where hay is kept

DOWN

1 Like Kia Souls
2 Brand that had a pink-and-green 2021 tie-in with Lady Gaga, and no, I didn't imagine it, that really happened
3 Slate of options at the dispensary
4 Mariner's guide
5 Trail mix alternative
6 Rio's Carnaval precedes it
7 Hippocratic ___
8 Green car that comes in many colors
9 Winston Churchill, politically
10 Mortal Kombat character with Elsa-like powers
11 Prince of "Aladdin"
12 Alphabetic trio
15 On this occasion, unlike previous occasions
20 Common connector
21 French king
24 When an attack is scheduled to start
25 Was given no choice
26 Samuel of America's highest court
27 Zest for life
28 "___ Boom" ("Waiting for Guffman" song)
30 Blues musician ___ Mo'
31 Sports replay technique
32 Emotionally detached
33 Carbonated debut of 2005
36 Gumbo vegetable
39 Ready to rock and/or roll
40 High crime
45 They say it makes the heart grow fonder, but I've also heard it makes the heart to wander
48 ___ cable (Best Buy purchase)
50 "What You ___" (61-Down song)
51 Respond to a busy signal, perhaps
53 Make into law
55 Like some games
56 "Just doin' my job"
57 Minnesota Representative Ilhan
58 "My Life and the Beautiful Game" autobiographer
59 Home to Vigeland Park
60 Animated snowman who says he "likes warm hugs"
61 One of 10 musicals to win the Pulitzer Prize for Drama
62 "___ Mine" (Beatles song)
63 Huck's friend

YOUNG AT HEART

BY ADESINA O. KOIKI

ACROSS

1 Motown legend Ross
6 "48 Hrs." actor Nick
11 "___ inside" (convenience store sign)
14 Luxury hotel amenities
15 Ancient Roman music hall
16 Greek X
17 "Psych!" (I always thought it was "Sike!" growing up, however)
19 Hi-___ image
20 2020 Pixar film
21 Dairy farm residents
22 "Aladdin" treasure
26 Country song that hit #1 twice, most recently in a 1983 version by Charley Pride
30 Pet shop lizard
32 18-Down, por ejemplo
33 "Grown Ups" actress Maria
34 "This is exactly how I feel," in some social media shares
35 Shortest radius of an ellipse
41 ___ Hunt (one half of a seminal Nintendo double feature)
42 Provoked a strong feeling in
44 Rude reply
47 NASA outfits
48 Make a document no longer secret
51 Word after litmus or stress
52 All-in-one Apple computer
53 Extremely urgent
55 Conjunction paired with neither
56 Vehement denial
63 ___-El (Superman's Kryptonian name)
64 San Diego State University athlete
65 Long for enviously
66 Nonspecific choice
67 Expression of exasperation
68 Call made by team captains before football games

DOWN

1 ABA/NBA legend Erving, to basketball fans
2 Letters noting a debt
3 "Washboard" muscles
4 Part of a Ping-Pong table (You call it table tennis? So be it!)
5 Inquires
6 "Thanks, Captain Obvious!"
7 In a strange manner
8 Floral necklace
9 One is 2,000 pounds
10 Subject with vocabulary: Abbr.
11 Old TV's "Three's ___"
12 Music group that performed at halftime of Super Bowl XLIV in 2010
13 "Get Ur Freak On" rapper Elliott
18 Des Moines is its capital
21 "Peace out," chatroom style
22 Ad-___
23 Quite a long, long time
24 Proverbial embodiment of stubbornness
25 Word before Sunday or Beach
27 Politician O'Rourke
28 Sensation-producing genre that's a sensation on YouTube: Abbr.
29 Second-string units
31 "Beats me!"
34 Publicity, metaphorically
36 British mothers
37 Completes, as a cake
38 Delete using two strokes
39 Jazz vocalist Anderson, a staple in shows alongside Duke Ellington
40 Tennis or volleyball match units
43 "Spring ahead" clock hours: Abbr.
44 Voice displeasure over
45 2007–12 Nickelodeon sitcom starring Miranda Cosgrove
46 R&B trio with hits including "Waterfalls" and "No Scrubs"
47 Sandwich topped with tzatziki
48 Tribe of Sudan's Nile basin
49 Waits at a drive-thru, say
50 Abercrombie & ___
54 Engrave
56 Baled fodder
57 Sleep-___ (nighttime product)
58 Abbreviation seen on corners of most cell phones nowadays (assuming you're not using Wi-Fi)
59 Basic gardening tool
60 Perón or Longoria
61 Homer's cartoon neighbor
62 Periods in which ties are broken: Abbr.

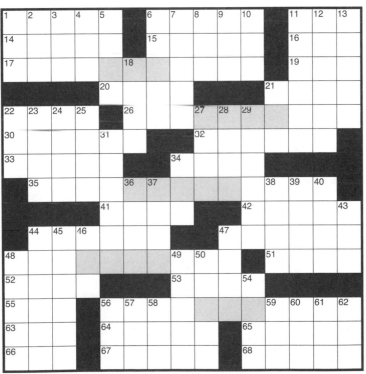

ORIGIN STORY

BY WILL NEDIGER

ACROSS

1 LSD
5 Warning signs in shark attack movies
9 "As if!"
13 It makes the earth move
14 Cookie after which a Fran Ross novel is named
15 Potatoes, in South Asian cuisine
16 Doing some legislative work?
18 Knit one, ___ two
19 Bird's primary instrument
20 Tres menos uno
22 "Life Goes On" K-pop band
23 Smoke accompaniment
24 Owl costume?
26 Daycare charges
27 Ernesto Guevara's nickname
29 Magazine with an iconic yellow border, casually
30 "1000 Forms of Fear" singer
31 Award-winnning Spanish actress Carmen
33 ___ face
34 Poultry farmer?
36 Rugby pileup
39 Desperate entreaties
40 Something to hold down
43 Mild, light cigars
45 Dance move often performed by politicians trying to seem cool
46 Big name in tomb-raiding
47 Beat poetry, in the '50s?
49 Scottish title-holders
51 Diamond judge
52 Bollywood superstar Aishwarya
53 Faux pas at the dinner table
54 Accumulation during a vacation
56 Song from Disney's "Hercules," or a hint to this puzzle's theme entries
58 Sicily's highest peak
59 Alternate name for Jerusalem
60 Recovers from trauma
61 Partners of rules, briefly
62 Toy that can "sleep"
63 Woody's owner in "Toy Story"

DOWN

1 First planned mission of NASA's Moon landing program
2 Choral work with instrumental accompaniment
3 Potential pitfalls for translators
4 Hard to get through
5 People, in a spelling meant to signal inclusiveness
6 Certain savings plan, briefly
7 Makeover component
8 "Leaving already?"
9 ___ smear
10 Targets of seasonal vaccines
11 Decade when Tupperware was invented
12 Karenina's creator
13 Mine passages
17 Accessory for some lawnmowers
21 What's wagered
24 Proclaims
25 Pancake recipe verb
28 Dromedary feature
31 Margo Jefferson's "Negroland," e.g.
32 On the briny
34 Throw with great force
35 Device with a touchscreen
36 Amy with the standup special "Mostly Sex Stuff"
37 Atmosphere
38 Spitting bars
40 Marine Corps member, slangily
41 Not chaotic
42 Low-voiced singers
44 Super stylish
46 Growth on a rock
48 "Old MacDonald" refrain
50 Key concept in Hawaiian culture
53 "Pride (In the Name of Love)" singer
55 ___ Vegas
57 Activist and author Arundhati

INDIVIDUAL RIGHTS

BY ANDREW J. RIES

ACROSS

1 Oinker's home
4 Where a liner might be found
9 The "A" of WASP
14 Football supporter
15 "___ got to be kiddin' me!"
16 Attempted to attract
17 Some window inserts: Abbr.
18 Cheat an infamous Chicago gangster out of money?
20 "Another example which illustrates the point"
22 Bogged down
23 Concave type of navel
24 Don't just dislike
25 Comic Dillon
28 Computer programmer's lines created anew?
31 Factor in a horror film's rating, maybe
32 Deodorant brand that's French for "tough"
33 Ingredient that turns a liquor into a liqueur

34 Punk musician Dee Dee doing a fried chicken step?
40 Raging mad
41 Org. that protects against workplace discrimination
42 Numbers of interest in sports betting
43 Become an expert at making cornbread?
49 Franchise with a short-lived "Cyber" spin-off
50 Barbecue joint freebies
51 Warm glows
52 Softens the difficulty of, in slang
54 Blustery talk

56 Realm filled with a pale blue gas?
59 JFK force
60 Last letter in an alphabet
61 It's not original programming
62 Take in some calories
63 Exposed
64 Title character in a Disney film
65 Hoops great Bird

DOWN

1 Unchanging
2 Genre related to electronica
3 Improv comedy rule that keeps the bit going
4 Breeding ground for certain mollusks

5 Tennis player Gauff
6 Currency used in 20 countries
7 St. crosser
8 "Seinfeld" character whose first name was never divulged
9 Cognizant
10 "Uh-uh"
11 All set
12 Director Wiseman
13 Poet's creation
19 Refer to
21 Item with bow and string varieties
24 Measurable quality of peppers
26 Key party in the JCPOA
27 Simple
29 Make a goof

30 Result of failing a breath test: Abbr.
31 Minty strip, maybe
33 One of seven in Catholicism
34 Coalition
35 Gives assistance to
36 Meal consumed in a den, say
37 "___ the season ..."
38 Jordan Peele film title starter
39 Lumpsucker eggs
43 Offend
44 Act like a sponge
45 Drinking establishment
46 Gives a blustery talk
47 Capital of the Bahamas
48 Swanky residence
50 Like low humor
53 Advantage
54 When repeated, part of the Leeward Islands
55 Heavy load
56 Soft toss
57 Org. for a physician
58 Last letter in an alphabet

25

IT'S NOT EASY BEING 39-ACROSS

BY PATRICK BLINDAUER

ACROSS

1 Light course
6 New Orleans sandwich
11 Report card fig.
14 Pitch-changing guitar clamps
15 Take the honey and run?
16 Tayback who played Mel on "Alice"
17 Atmospheric causes of climate change
19 "Crasswords" constructor Dunbar
20 ___ one's stuff
21 Recoiled in fear
23 "I Won't Send ___" (Jerry Herman song)
26 Mating game?
27 Colorful stuff used to make cave paintings
31 "Freeze!"
32 ___ and dangerous
33 Resort in the Rockies
35 Tate collection
38 "High ___" (1952 Gary Cooper western)
39 Color represented by its first letter in the first box of 17-Across, 58-Across, 11-Down, and 29-Down
40 Ballpark figures, briefly
41 South African game
42 Flip over
43 Letter shaped like a triangle
44 Puppies' playful bites
46 With 24-Down, name of the collective ability used by colorful ursine creatures of the '80s
48 Patronize, as a restaurant
50 Red carpet walker, informally
51 Lady in "Lady and the Tramp," e.g.
53 Tend to the turkey, perhaps
57 Pod opening?
58 Wisconsin team
62 A, in German class
63 Capital once known as Thăng Long ("Ascending Dragon")
64 Vernacular
65 Ernie in the World Golf Hall of Fame
66 Major KFC supplier
67 Printer brand owned by Seiko

DOWN

1 Heart chart: Abbr.
2 Sounds from a satisfied customer
3 Help out, in a gym (so I hear)
4 "How to Train ___ Dragon"
5 One way to rest
6 Piece of a guitar or a cribbage set
7 End for pay or Cray
8 Pair of pears, perhaps
9 Letters under TUV, on classic phones
10 Words from a positive person
11 Spinach or broccoli, for example
12 Heaps
13 They're far from basic
18 School that's a music symbol in reverse
22 Org. of the Toronto Maple Leafs
24 See 46-Across
25 Magazine that honors Black women in Hollywood
27 Pain for one losing the hunger games?
28 Fe, chemically
29 Vermont range
30 Roughly half the world
31 Mother clucker
34 Put the ___ to the metal
36 Meter maid in a Beatles tune
37 Fabergé egg collector
39 Modern navigation aid, for short
40 Title for Tevye
42 Unable to relax
43 Total clusterfudge
45 McKellen of "X-Men"
47 Sitcom starring a Grammy-winning singer
48 Name associated with Clinique
49 Reporter Ryan
50 Scottish families
52 Auction site that I seem to be addicted to—yes, I do need that many board games!
54 Uno card verb
55 Hamiltonian papers, in a way
56 Logical Latin word
59 "___-hoo!"
60 It may be found in a cushion
61 Mama's boy

COVER ALL THE BASES

BY ADESINA O. KOIKI

ACROSS

1 Quixote companion
6 Brain fart
11 Cooking spray in a yellow can
14 Test or experiment
15 Cinema guide?
16 Game where stacking "Wild Draw Four" cards is illegal, going against everything many learned in school cafeterias
17 Health care program championed by Bernie Sanders
19 Messenger ___
20 A couple of bucks, say
21 Command seen on an email ribbon
22 Identify
23 Bazillion years
25 Without company
27 Villainous siblings from the '90s game show "Where in the World Is Carmen Sandiego?"
32 Energy-carrying molecule, briefly
33 Actor Morales
34 Constantly complains
37 Scan used to diagnose a torn ACL
38 English architectural style characterized by half-timbering
41 Gold medal–winning gymnast Raisman
42 Word after hot or fancy
45 Produced, as produce
47 Charged atom
48 European military alliance formed before World War I
52 Cousin of a vaquero
53 It was used to announce Michael Jordan's return to basketball in 1995 after his retirement two years prior
54 Nonbinary gender pronoun
55 "The Maltese Falcon" star Mary
58 "___ Don't Preach" (Madonna hit)
62 Ewe's bleat
63 Perform very successfully ... and what needs to be done to complete this puzzle's "cycle"
65 Compete in a super-G
66 New Balance competitor
67 Company's public perception
68 ___ excellence
69 "Ditto!"
70 Cornered

DOWN

1 Psychological condition sometimes treated with ecstasy: Abbr.
2 R&B singer India.___
3 Number of playable areas in tic-tac-toe
4 Croatian capital
5 Word used after a number to indicate a tie
6 "Kick, Push" rapper ___ Fiasco
7 At once, in memos
8 Greek pastry in thin sheets
9 Informal goodbye
10 Do wrong
11 1984 Academy Award winner for Best Original Song Score
12 Irk
13 Watery castle protector
18 Hemingway or Borgnine
22 Actress Ward
24 ___ Miss
26 Where the pro football contest infamously known as the "Heidi Game" aired
27 Like towel-dried hair
28 Other: Spanish
29 Pending
30 T, to Greeks
31 Narrow hilltop
35 It may thicken, in a mystery
36 "Auld Lang ___"
39 Wash. neighbor
40 Mel ___, Hall-of-Fame defensive back and Dallas Cowboys great
43 Airplane seat feature
44 Title for seven-time Formula One title winner Lewis Hamilton
46 Venus is a member of it: Abbr.
49 Adulation
50 Blew a gasket
51 One type of witness
52 "I'm Every Woman" singer Khan
54 Cooking measurement: Abbr.
56 Food associated with Tuesday
57 Extremely
59 The "A" in UAE
60 Treeless plateau of the Andes
61 Gibb who wasn't in the Bee Gees
63 Attention hog ... or meat from a hog
64 Degree held by many CEOs

KIN SELECTION

BY WILL NEDIGER

ACROSS

1 Doesn't zig
5 Country whose Azure Window collapsed in 2017
10 "Lupin" star ___ Sy
14 Zone
15 Times for divas to shine
16 Name in the corner of many YouTube videos
17 Nap kin?
19 French friends
20 Off-limits actions
21 Keto or paleo
23 Enjoy some larb, e.g.
24 Hockey infraction
25 Munch kin?
27 Work well together
28 Country where Vox Media is based
30 Organized ___
31 Learned
35 Shutterbugs' purchases: Abbr.
36 Pump kin?
38 Honeys
40 Couturiers' creations
41 Blasé feeling
43 Caustic substance
44 Claimed ability that skeptics look askance at
47 Push kin?
51 Medication for cramps
53 Something to seize
54 Like a wet noodle
55 Get to know people at a mixer
56 Singer from County Donegal
58 Bump kin?
60 Perched on
61 São ___
62 Landlord's extraction
63 Go back for another tour of duty
64 Along for the ride
65 Wild display

DOWN

1 Voluptuous
2 Someone who doesn't experience romantic or sexual attraction, for short
3 Exercise wheel user
4 Didn't reveal
5 Gaping mouths
6 Grande, to fans
7 Cardellini of "Freaks and Geeks"
8 Snack with Fuego and Xplosion flavors
9 Good thing to have
10 Egg cells
11 Ripe for online mockery
12 Amelia Earhart, e.g.
13 Fantasy sports lineups
18 Cultured fare
22 Up to, briefly
25 Abuelo's daughter
26 Chooses actors for
29 Took to court
31 Follow
32 Part of the Department of the Treasury: Abbr.
33 Twilled fabric
34 Like French toast
36 Jealous words
37 Needing iron supplements
38 Lead-in to a request for a favor
39 Slowish, on a score
42 Not online, briefly
44 More envelope-pushing
45 "Bye for now!"
46 Abundance
48 Hedren of "Marnie"
49 Former Pakistani prime minister (and former cricket star) Khan
50 "I'm a Little Teapot" word
52 101 course
55 "Gimme some cat treats!"
57 "There's an ___ for that"
59 "Hustlers" co-star, casually

SPOKEN WORD GENRES

BY ANDREW J. RIES

ACROSS

1 Catch red-handed
5 Tom who's played in a record 10 Super Bowls
10 Letter before Quebec in the NATO alphabet
14 Female youth org.
15 Zodiac sign symbolized by the scales
16 Piece of news
17 Show toughness, say
20 Brimming-with-energy types
21 Cummerbunds and obis, for example
22 Snap out of it
25 Singer Carly ___ Jepsen
26 Splash against, as waves
29 Sheet that clings
33 Stop dreaming
35 Some afternoon rechargers
36 Roger or Brian of ambient music fame
37 Naked
38 Raptor center resident
40 Waiting room array, for short
41 A king or queen may have one named for them
42 Landing spot on a lake
43 Devices that might be light-emitting
45 Fish with a fruit in its name
48 Holmes maker
49 April standard in Annapolis: Abbr.
50 Fonda's co-star on "Grace and Frankie"
52 Away from the bow, on a ship
55 Personal information
59 Best Picture winner set in Austria ... and a hint to the last words of 17-, 29-, and 45-Across
62 Not only mine
63 ___ pan (ring-shaped cookware)
64 Riverbed deposit
65 Plateau-like landform
66 Doesn't bolt
67 Bits of skin art, say

DOWN

1 Big Apple force: Abbr.
2 Off course
3 Widely recognized celebrity
4 Dessert with a core of molten chocolate
5 Develop into a flower
6 Does a dishwashing step
7 Suga succeeded him as prime minister of Japan
8 Some medical drama characters: Abbr.
9 Veggies high in potassium
10 Lumber yard cutter
11 Prepared for immediate action
12 He was named FIFA's Player of the Century in 2000
13 Iowa State University city
18 Don't act subtly
19 Merits
23 Hybrid in the produce section
24 Word-of-mouth
26 Pop bottle sheath
27 Conscious of the situation
28 Boundaries that define ranges
30 Did an imitation of
31 Halo wearer
32 Gang in a western film
34 Loch with a famed monster
39 Very much
40 Granular lunar material
42 Host's starting performance
44 You shouldn't take it literally
46 Texas city named for a Ukrainian seaport
47 Personify
51 Elevators in the U.K.
52 Target of scientific splitting
53 Elisabeth of "The Boys"
54 Dog bone remnants
56 Mongolia's home
57 Lean to one side
58 Variety show series
60 Bolt go-with
61 Genetic substance

GEM CLASS

BY PATRICK BLINDAUER

ACROSS

1 Cause of friend-influenced choices
6 Mexican bread
11 What we called my 6th-grade science teacher, since Brewinski was too tricky to say, I guess
14 Recipient of many prayers
15 Like some change
16 Editor's add-on?
17 It's far from forte, musically
18 Jamaican who follows Jah
19 Peeples of "Fame" fame
20 Certain swingers
22 Maker of big bucks
24 Suffix for some sugars
25 Part of iOS: Abbr.
27 Estrada of "CHiPs"
28 Chiefs' div.
32 Cockpit gauge setting
34 Bring up the rear?
35 Designer known for her wedding gowns
38 Mr. Potato Head piece
39 What pressure + coal = 4 times in this puzzle's grid
41 Word repeated before Dolls
43 Sporadically
45 Name shared by 12 popes
46 Place to apply shiatsu
47 Lines intersecting curves, in geometry
50 "Jeopardy!" creator Griffin
51 Oingo Boingo's "Only a ___ "
54 Certain camera type: Abbr.
55 Prefix with state or stellar
57 What the first number represents in a certain diagnostic test
62 Agatha Christie, ___ Miller
63 Submit an online return
65 Understood without being said
66 Make a typo, for exmaple
67 Home of the Nubian Desert
68 Cackling carnivore
69 Blog feed format, for short
70 Reznor who co-wrote ambient music for "Soul"
71 NutriBullet alternative

DOWN

1 Joseph who brought Shakespeare to Central Park
2 "Night" Nobelist Wiesel
3 Stylish elegance
4 Chased, as a suspect
5 "Ragtime" protagonist Walker
6 Home of the volcano El Misti
7 Reasons to cram
8 Mouthing off
9 10, at times: Abbr.
10 "He would ___ his best friend for the sake of writing an epigram on his tombstone": Oscar Wilde
11 Taking, as a secondary course of study
12 Coming down on and canceling
13 Bituminous stuff
21 "___ Misérables"
23 Dolly inducted her into the Country Music Hall of Fame
26 Give the once-over
28 Dr.'s order?
29 To begin with
30 Duvets
31 Spot on the tube
33 System that uses four tires at once: Abbr.
36 Offshoot of punk
37 Hollywood's Howard and Perlman
39 Fogelberg of folk
40 Not domestic, as a flight: Abbr.
42 WWII spy gp.
44 Orange pool ball number
45 Combination bets
46 One who works a shaft shift
48 Ballpark figure: Abbr.
49 Fate who spins the thread of life
52 Comment whispered to the audience
53 "Like a Rolling Stone" songwriter Bob
56 Metered marking of silence
58 ___ packing (dismissed)
59 "Law & Order: SVU" actor
60 Movie theater, in Madrid
61 Medicated shampoo additive
64 ___ baby (pet)

TELL ME THE BACKSTORY

BY ADESINA O. KOIKI

ACROSS

1 O and OWN founder
6 Hangout for ducks or frogs
10 "Get a ___!"
14 "___ on!" (Catchphrase uttered by a member of Marvel Comics' Fantastic Four)
15 Repeat the arguments of
16 Mystical glow
17 Whistleblower
19 Wheat pasta used in Japanese cuisine
20 Brian who was briefly in Roxy Music
21 "Hamilton" event between Burr and Hamilton
22 Jerry Maguire's occupation in "Jerry Maguire"
23 Film category that includes surrealist cinema
27 67-Across, en español
28 "Star Wars" queen
32 Disciple of Socrates who taught Aristotle
35 Amenity at an upscale hotel
36 Red letters?
37 Social media footprint since 2004
42 Variety of evergreen tree
43 Vera Atkins or Virginia Hall, during World War II
44 "Delta of Venus" author Nin
45 Molasses, to Brits
48 Erstwhile laundry detergent brand (Tsk, tsk, tsk if you don't know it!)
50 Percussion instrument similar to a xylophone
55 Boutique, e.g.
58 Suffix with million or Frigid
59 Nike's ___-FIT fabric
60 Goad
61 Confidential scheme
64 Like a hamburger that's still mooing
65 Advanced in years
66 "Kids ___ days ..."
67 A starfish has at least five of them
68 Fluctuate
69 A source of pillow feathers

DOWN

1 Quite a lot
2 Texas city northeast of Dallas
3 Boca ___, Florida
4 Quantity: Abbr.
5 Retained employment
6 Bernadette of Broadway
7 Florida city known as the "Horse Capital of the World"
8 Gp. featuring the Wild, Panthers, Predators, and Sharks
9 Name of anonymity
10 Sized up
11 "That was uncalled for!"
12 Proverbial self-sharpener
13 Short, quick breath
18 ___ 2020 (continental soccer event actually held in 2021)
22 MP4 alternative
24 A student may pass it
25 Snack of Spanish cuisine
26 Apple computer available in seven colors
29 H_2O, south of the border
30 Anderson of "WKRP in Cincinnati"
31 Many New Yorkers live in them: Abbr.
32 Deflating noise
33 Villain's stereotypical hideout
34 Rural land measurement
35 Chicago's WNBA team
38 Norwegian capital
39 Crude group?
40 Old media storage format
41 Like privates peeling potatoes, probably
46 Sides (with)
47 Largest airport in Ohio: Abbr.
48 Creepy individual, colloquially
49 Legal memo header
51 Grammy-winning country singer Musgraves
52 Spent time doing nothing
53 Irregular or uneven
54 Size of cola requested in a "Super Troopers" scene at a burger joint
55 Totally convinced (of)
56 Ice cube container
57 Shrek, e.g.
61 "___ My Name" (1999 Destiny's Child hit)
62 It can be bruised or inflated
63 Φ

31

KITCHEN ISLANDS

BY WILL NEDIGER

ACROSS

1 Morehouse or Fisk, for short
5 Scrabble tile holders
10 Vegetarian gelatin substitute
14 Greek equivalent of Cupid
15 "Gesundheit!" elicitor
16 ___ your time
17 Light green nuts
19 Even once
20 Good-looking
21 Hair care brand that makes Pro-V
23 Low-pH substances
24 "The Devil Wears ___"
26 "Galang" rapper
27 Psychoactive chemical in cannabis
28 Double-reed instruments
30 Mixture of spices
32 Crystal ball user
34 Inc. relative
35 Lightly throws
36 Chinese steamed buns
39 Share a tweet on Facebook, e.g.
41 Henry ___ (first Tudor monarch)
42 "Birdhouse in Your Soul" band, briefly
45 Big name in violin-making
46 Dutch city known for blue and white pottery
48 ___ of Good Feelings
49 Can, with or without "can"
50 Love to bits
52 Type of tea from India
54 Substance in many murder mysteries
56 Driver of gentrification
57 Part that wags
58 Bread often topped with cheese
61 Gold piece?
62 Come in
63 Slush Puppie cousin
64 Canadian bills that depict Viola Desmond
65 Stately mount
66 "___ is a bore" (Robert Venturi's architectural maxim)

DOWN

1 Jazz aficionados, back in the day
2 Eggy French bread
3 Process in which the universe changes scale
4 "Tú" alternative
5 Not appropriate for kids, perhaps
6 Hanover "Oh no!"
7 Greek letter used to abbreviate "Christ"
8 "Mario Kart" creatures with dangerous shells
9 "What a pity!"
10 Aid and ___
11 "I need time alone"
12 DNA component along with guanine, cytosine, and thymine
13 Enjoys again, as a favorite book
18 "Oh, and another thing ..."
22 Bigwig
24 Way to gather opinions
25 Bounce back
29 Stain on one's reputation
31 Exam which you can take up to seven times
33 Revolutionary activity
35 "The workweek's over!"
37 ___ elephant
38 River with "white" and "blue" tributaries
39 Rapping sound
40 One of seven in the UAE
43 Sears and then cooks at a simmer
44 Sex cells
46 Museum educator
47 Adjective that often describes thrillers
51 Thin mint products
53 Ruin, as a twist
55 Central Park trees
56 Where Kelis's milkshake brings all the boys
59 4G ___
60 Flying buzzers

MAY FIRST

BY ANDREW J. RIES

ACROSS

1 Four duos create one
6 ___ land (dream world)
10 Synonymous rhyme of "grab"
13 Common expression of disbelief on TikTok
14 Like many Etsy offerings
15 Unneeded hubbub
16 Not-so-humble abode
17 Bricklayer's levy?
19 One of the Twelve Olympians
20 Small handful
22 Summertime weather descriptor
23 Studio time with the "Mad Love" pop star?
27 Fashion designer who co-wrote "The Natty Professor"
28 Sleeveless bedwear, for short
32 The "P" of PBR
35 With 43-Across, grid of numbers illustrating a sports transaction?
37 A Zamboni drives on it
38 Bleating mother
41 "Tamerlane and Other Poems" author, whose name is hidden in this clue
42 Clumsy sort
43 See 35-Across
46 Metallic-sounding, perhaps
48 TV host Banks
49 Array at a bar
52 Container for keeping cosmetics?
57 Steer clear of
60 Intent
61 Personal helper
62 Bill for buying a certain kind of syrup?
65 Tops
67 Ace's value, often
68 Community center fixture
69 Was a curator for
70 Comic/physician Jeong
71 Moppet
72 Microsoft Office component

DOWN

1 Catherine who has frequently co-starred with Eugene Levy
2 A-lister, perhaps
3 Collections used at afternoon socials
4 Top-left key on a keyboard
5 Godly conviction
6 Annuity alternative
7 Butterfield of "Sex Education"
8 "___ Demoiselles d'Avignon" (Picasso painting)
9 Marinade in Spanish cooking
10 Countrywide: Abbr.
11 Genesis frontman?
12 Crate-shaped
13 Fraudulent offers and such
18 Grammy-winning folkie Griffith
21 "Family Guy" girl
24 Soda size
25 Break under pressure
26 Digging
29 Nerve cell projection
30 Gripe
31 Not at all reliable
32 University in the Steel City, commonly
33 Like sore muscles
34 PBR, for example
36 Looking past?
39 Unhurried gait
40 "Tommy" star Falco
44 Language spoken in Sri Lanka
45 Even-keeled in temperament
47 Word in the official name of Iran
50 Wire letters
51 Amount of resistance
53 Like a dab hand
54 Two-terminal electrical tube
55 Auto flop of note
56 Emeritus, for short
57 Run ___
58 Low-tech weather device
59 Sign at a shop
63 Many a stocking stuffer
64 Just super
66 Wedding rental, for short

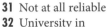

33

BULL SESSION

BY PATRICK BLINDAUER

ACROSS

1 They show you what's where
5 PS5 button
10 "Yikes!"
14 Giant Jesus of the '60s
15 Surprise Oscar winner of the '90s
16 Model of iPod
17 Get on the Chicago ballplayer's shoulders?
19 Put away for later
20 Ed Asner's role in "Elf"
21 Speed-of-sound breaker at JFK, once
22 Pet ___
23 Stressful high-school event
25 "Moby-Dick" narrator
27 Badmouth the Chicago ballplayer?
31 Insect that takes power naps
32 Distance between wing tips
33 Georgia's capital: Abbr.
34 Winter fort material
36 Train, truck, or tractor, at times
38 "One-___ Jacks" (1961 Brando film)
42 Hard-rock connection?
45 Held onto
48 Cry at the World Cup
49 Douse the flaming Chicago ballplayer?
54 Showers, for example
55 Robert who played A.J. on "The Sopranos"
56 Like neon and argon
57 CPAs crunch them: Abbr.
60 Luggage attachment
63 Strike zone, in a way
64 Give special treatment to the Chicago ballplayer?
66 "The Wizard of ___" (short-lived game show)
67 Stay away from
68 One of Pakistan's official languages
69 "Hey, wait up you ___!"
70 2016 winner of the Nobel Prize in Literature
71 Buzzing nuisance

DOWN

1 Big Sur runners
2 "It's ___ big misunderstanding!"
3 Identifies, in a way
4 Fort where the Civil War began
5 When you can expect a touchdown: Abbr.
6 Classified information?
7 Creatures on Australian coins
8 Welsh's language family
9 Up to, briefly
10 Complete outfit
11 French sponge cake
12 Words after many works of fiction
13 Succeed
18 They may be stolen
22 Baby ___ Beauty
24 About five mL
26 Penn in Manhattan, for one: Abbr.
27 Some "Law & Order" figs.
28 Retirement spot, say
29 Morita of "The Karate Kid"
30 Sushi bar mushroom
35 Sara Bareilles musical based on a 2007 film
37 Word that may accompany an affirmative action
39 "I'm done playing"
40 Capital of Luxembourg?
41 Director Guillermo ___ Toro
43 Tiny tantrum
44 Basis for some discrimination
46 Upsilon's follower
47 Shire with no connection to "The Lord of the Rings," as far as I can tell
49 Literary conclusion
50 Movie musical that won the first Worst Director Razzie Award
51 All the rage
52 Seals are part of it
53 Parasite that's a member of the genus Cimex
58 Planetary path, usually
59 Slice, Squirt, or Jolt
61 Director of the last "M*A*S*H" episode
62 Overabundance
64 Supplied with Cheese Puffs, e.g.
65 Stimpy's foil

HEAVY METAL

BY Adesina O. Koiki

ACROSS

1 "World of Warcraft" and others, briefly
5 "Terrible" toddler's age
8 Covered with prickles
13 404 ___
15 Address with dots
16 Like a beaver, it is said
17 Jeweler's magnifying glass
18 Sources of valuable information
20 Resistant to illness
22 Connection
23 Tree with purplish-brown leaves
25 Shakshuka ingredient
28 Exclamation popularized by pro wrestling legend Ric Flair
29 Alvin ___, New Orleans Saints running back and 5× Pro Bowler
31 Penn or Grand Central, in NYC
34 Home improvement acronym
36 Assigns stars, say
37 Of little importance
41 Sun-related prefix
42 Part of TTYL
43 "Game of Thrones" patriarch Stark
44 "No treat for you!"
46 2010 #1 hit for Usher and will.i.am
48 Adoration in verse
49 Metaphor for a failure
56 Subtle insult
57 Voiced a refusal
58 Attractive older gentleman
62 Everything bagels are covered in them
63 Scornful glance
64 Tonsillitis specialist: Abbr.
65 Figure out, like this clue
66 Justin, Lance, Joey, JC, and Chris (1995–2002)
67 Key used to make an exit?
68 Playoff round permanently instituted before 1994's strike-shortened baseball season (though not played that year): Abbr.

DOWN

1 Item from long ago
2 Type of code, for short
3 Sourpuss
4 Absorb
5 Give a hard yank
6 Penned
7 Basic skateboarding trick
8 Like Havarti or Gouda
9 It's weakness leaving the body, in a motivational platitude
10 Video game news website
11 Formerly, matrimonially
12 Age measures: Abbr.
14 Extend a membership
19 Cruise ship floor
21 Decay over time
24 Instruction for cooking a 25-Across, perhaps
25 Words on a Wonderland cake
26 Avarice
27 ___ guzzler
30 Important street name
31 Golfer Sam with a PGA Tour record 82 victories
32 Jalapeño feature?
33 ___ reflux (heartburn causer)
35 "I'm so excited!"
38 Disc jockey known as the father of hip-hop
39 Total beginner, slangily
40 "The Three Musketeers" novelist Alexandre
41 "Game of Thrones" network
45 "Get your ass in ___!"
47 Wine-tasting need
50 Cost for a TV spot
51 Filmmaker Taylor and chemist Miles
52 Rest atop, as a bed
53 Former "Entertainment Tonight" host Nancy
54 How some TV series are sold
55 Scent-detecting organs
56 Reindeer in "Frozen"
58 Nine-digit ID: Abbr.
59 Connections
60 Longtime ESPN anchor Bob
61 British new wave band whose name sounds like a street drug

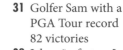

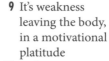

LETTER SHAPES

BY WILL NEDIGER

ACROSS

1 Erotica, derogatorily
5 "The Country Girls" author O'Brien
9 Say, "Yeah, I bet"
14 Lose on purpose
15 Dress like, at a Halloween party
16 Cause of sleeplessness
17 "... approximately"
18 Darkwave listener, maybe
19 Two-for-one deal, e.g.
20 Pianist Alice Sara ___
21 Musical ending
22 Heath bar base
23 1D shape, both geometrically and orthographically
26 Record of a single year
27 Speed ___
28 Gradually goes down
32 Counterpart of a yoni, in Hinduism
34 Little ___ ("Grey Gardens" figure, familiarly)
36 Country with seven sheikhs, briefly
37 Sash for a kimono
38 2D shape, both geometrically and orthographically
40 Screening org.
41 Britton who had an affair with Warren G. Harding
42 It gets the grease
43 Jake ___ (Jack Nicholson's role in "Chinatown")
45 Therefore
47 Part of an office tangle
49 Workout program with a portmanteau name
50 3D shape, both geometrically and orthographically

53 Big books
56 (Pay) attention
57 Substance collected from maples
58 Figurative turn of phrase
59 "Curses!"
60 Bit of Turkish cash
61 Absorb with a piece of bread
62 Privy to
63 "What are the ___?"
64 Absolutely terrible
65 One of the sixteen Decade Volcanoes
66 What you might settle for

DOWN

1 Had no peers
2 Place that stocks a lot of olives
3 Deciding to stop supporting as a fan
4 Ref's declaration in the ring
5 Goad into action
6 Thingamajig
7 Rock musician who fronted 10,000 Maniacs
8 Bonfire remnants
9 Have an attack of Bieber fever?
10 Classic first-date option
11 "Carmina Burana" composer
12 Not busy right now
13 Disastrous 2017 festival
21 Piña ___
22 Bathroom flooring, often
24 Running ___

25 Director Aldo whose first name is an anagram of his last name
29 Part of your toast that you hope lands up
30 Pieces of molding near the floor
31 Regular visitor's purchase
33 Romantic gifts that were popular in the 2000s
35 Not raw
39 Plant with many medicinal uses
44 Small amount
46 Despicable
48 Mailer-___ (sender of bounce messages)
51 Sex appeal
52 Beard dye for some Muslims
53 Something to shake while yelling "Get off my lawn!"
54 Smell
55 "Boys Will Be Boys" singer Dua
59 Run out of juice
60 Alternative to a laugh react

MAKE IT A DOUBLE

BY ANDREW J. RIES

ACROSS

1 Free-for-all
6 Title for Joan Collins and Diana Rigg
10 Frothy head
14 Free-for-all
15 Fairy tale beast
16 Field of energy around a person
17 Served from a keg, as beer
18 Tactic by one playing the blame game
20 *"Twistin' the Night Away" or "Wonderful World"?*
22 Factually correct
23 Bird that might be "bald"
27 Purchase at a bulk retailer
30 *Animated version of Humpty Dumpty, perhaps?*
34 Some geometry class calculations
36 Italian or French bread
37 Blue
38 Punch onomatopoeia
39 *Owl's home?*
42 Fertility clinic supply
43 Have regrets about
44 Tons
45 Sneakers' undersides
47 *Basketball target for a castaway?*
51 Snack between meals
52 Alabama setting of a namesake 2014 film
53 ___ Punk
55 Best International Feature Oscar winner in 2021 ... and what's been added to the italicized clues' answers
62 Parlor creations
65 Sleeping issue
66 Treat offered in a Java Chip flavor
67 Nights before
68 Spotify competitor
69 Southernmost of the Ivies
70 Mardi Gras city, informally
71 Set of twenty

DOWN

1 College hotshot's initialism
2 Nevada city near Lake Tahoe
3 Highish choir voice
4 Unconvincing argument, in slang
5 Social outcast
6 Crooked feature on a golf course
7 Spanish for "water"
8 Picture-taking medical procedures
9 Indie band with a "fishy" name
10 Rhyming term for a rich person
11 "Now is the winter of ___ discontent made glorious summer ...": "Richard III"
12 "Bussit" singer Lennox
13 Reference in an open-world video game
19 Vital parts of automotive steering systems
21 Stick in a pool hall
24 Leave the band
25 Units at a bakery
26 Punctuation mark similar to a hyphen
27 Pants that extend to the shins
28 Excite
29 Anna whose "Black Beauty" was the only novel she wrote
31 Really bother
32 Recipe's "c."
33 Constellation with a palindromic name
35 Woodstock group that parodied '50s music
40 Aged
41 "How interesting!"
46 Not drifting, in a way
48 Longest river in South America
49 Port on the Black Sea
50 Disc golfer's standard
54 Makeup of a college town "row"
56 Good sign for a shopper
57 Pioneer in DVR technology
58 Antagonist in pro wrestling
59 Reverse
60 Not far
61 Hill and ___
62 Soda, to most Midwesterners
63 State of anger
64 State of peace

HEAD GAMES

BY PATRICK BLINDAUER

ACROSS
1 Urban Dictionary entries
6 Oz creator L. Frank ___
10 Erie, for one
14 One working on pitches
15 Rubik, the cube maker
16 Tel ___
17 "Fear of Flying" author Jong
18 Not just skim
19 Make a mental ___
20 Minimization of potential business losses
23 Born, in marriage announcements
24 Two make a qt.
25 Apple on a desk, maybe
26 Prepares, as a fishhook
28 Grand Canyon, for one
32 Actress Mia of "Ferris Bueller's Day Off"

35 Headey of "Game of Thrones"
37 Country on the western side of Hispaniola
38 1991 Jackie Chan film
41 "In ___ we learn": George Herbert
42 Scrubbed, as a NASA mission
43 Stare in surprise
44 Short breathing cessation
45 40–40, to Venus
47 Village People hit of 1978
50 Vinyl, briefly
51 Morning lawn wetness
54 Fun person to be around
58 "Crucify" singer Amos
59 Italian dough, once

60 City that's also a poker variant
61 "Frozen" role
62 50% of sechs
63 Core belief
64 Window-shopping purchase?
65 Prediction maker
66 Nasal noise

DOWN
1 Not at all lenient
2 Novelist Alison, whose name becomes actor Hugh if you add an A
3 Ouzo component
4 Flamingo feature
5 Pop's pop
6 Leonard whose "Mass" opened the Kennedy Center
7 Office space calculation
8 Eel, at a sushi bar
9 Internet connection device
10 Highway maneuver
11 "Bard of ___ calling!" (How Shakespeare might introduce himself)
12 Talking car on "Knight Rider"
13 Apple consumer of note
21 Slightly cockeyed
22 "___ Man" (Village People hit of 1978)
26 Mayberry deputy
27 Hair net
29 Slave of opera
30 Word on an octagonal sign

31 Muck's partner
32 Singapore sling ingredient
33 Each, pricewise
34 It will hold your horses
36 Type of thin pasta
39 Best effort, athletically
40 Two-door automobile
46 Hundreds, in 1-Across
48 Viral infections
49 Smoking, probably
51 Liquid-Plumr competitor
52 Old anesthetic
53 Kurt's role in "Tombstone"
54 "Copacabana" showgirl
55 Turkey neighbor
56 Leopard's perch, perhaps
57 Grace period?
58 Dreidel, for one

PLACEHOLDERS

BY ADESINA O. KOIKI

ACROSS

1 There are four concerning thermodynamics
5 "___ and the Night Visitors"
10 CPR performers
14 Essayist Charles Lamb's pen name
15 Sasha's 13-Down
16 ___ Halliwell, a.k.a. "Ginger Spice"
17 1962 book of confessional poetry by Anne Sexton
20 Like some last words
21 Interruption
22 Thick sea fog that sounds like the start of a snarky laugh
23 Women's college basketball powerhouse with 11 national titles
25 Device sending electrical currents to body parts to relieve pain
31 Word after flight or credit
35 ___ gras
36 Consumed
37 Sign on for a tour of duty
39 "Good heavens!"
40 Popular brand of toilet paper
41 Water balloons, during a prank
44 Nonverbal agreements
45 Los Angeles–based streetwear brand founded in 2003
48 Freewheel
49 Workplace safety initials
53 Has a response
56 People mentioned in the Golden Rule
58 Stereotypical feature of an epic
61 Shortened engagement?
62 Bellowing
63 Macramé formation
64 Umpteen
65 Puts in order of preference
66 They're frequently popped on planes

DOWN

1 Bit of romaine
2 Subject of praise for over a billion people
3 ___ Rudolph, U.S. sprinter who won three gold medals at the 1960 Summer Olympics
4 Polynesian island group
5 Guitar Center buys
6 Tarnish
7 Blonde sitting at a bar?
8 Strike a chord
9 Sonia Sotomayor or Alexandria Ocasio-Cortez, e.g.
10 Showbiz grand slam, slangily
11 Link on a Yelp page
12 Spanish or French 101 word that's an anagram of 31-Down
13 Family nickname/palindrome
18 Asian nomad's circular tent
19 ___ Thigpen, former Steelers wide receiver and 2× Pro Bowler (1995, 1997)
23 Card game whose name is displayed on its playing cards
24 Forensic crime show franchise
26 Small amphibian
27 Actress Goldie
28 Langston Hughes poem associated with the Harlem Renaissance
29 Intelligent person, to haters
30 Means justifiers, it is said
31 Recharge batteries, perhaps
32 Unit for measuring bra size
33 ___ gin fizz
34 Friends and acquaintances
38 Plaster molding
39 Reddit administrator, for short
41 "To the stars," in Latin
42 "Scarecrow and ___ King" (1980s CBS spy series)
43 Encountered
46 Over the hill, in a sense
47 People who drink a lot
50 Harlem ___ (once-popular dance movement)
51 Source of red ink
52 Passionate feeling
53 ___ Nui (Easter Island)
54 "X Games" airer
55 DOJ employee
56 Yours and mine
57 Concordes, for example: Abbr.
58 FaceTime accessory
59 Bae alternative
60 Tree from an acorn

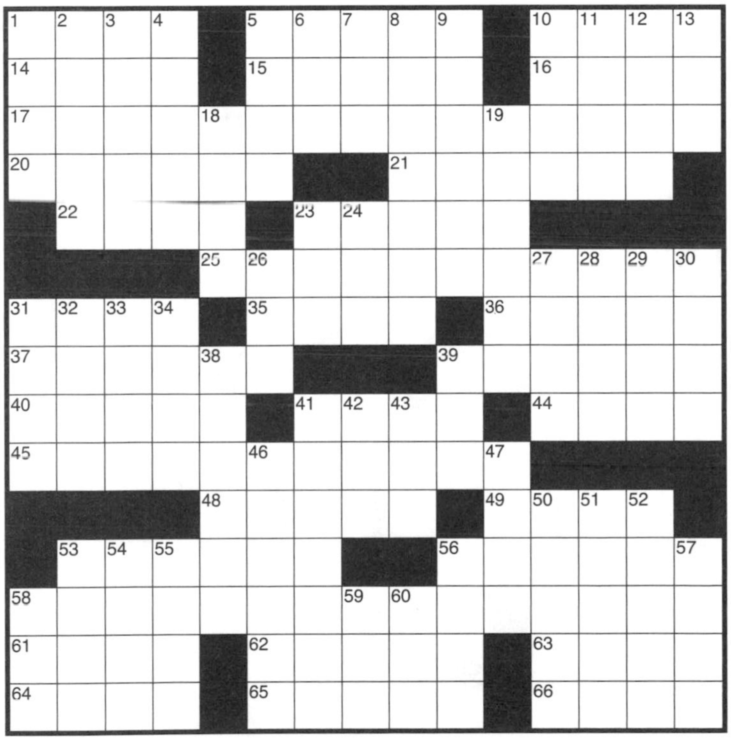

I'M UP

BY WILL NEDIGER

ACROSS

1 Kid's complaint when the internet is out
10 Pale lager, casually
14 Good for you
15 Deirdre McCloskey's field, for short
16 Plant with an almond-flavored custard named after it
18 Drive-___ window
19 Cutting corners, and more
20 Pickle herb
22 ___ chart (diagram with the CEO at the top)
23 Oscar de la ___
24 Director featured in Tananarive Due's UCLA course "The Sunken Place: Racism, Survival, and Black Horror Aesthetic"
25 Did a marathon
26 ___ Fletcher ("I've fallen, and I can't get up!" speaker)
27 Space station launched in 1986
29 Sailor, slangily
31 Squared off against
33 Garments often covered in flour
34 Curl up like a snake
37 Yiddish lament
39 Positive votes
40 ___ Way (Roman road)
42 Multigrain items?
44 Law
46 Classic name for a dog
47 No spring chicken
50 Tucked away
51 Event that might be protested by animal rights groups
53 In accordance with
55 Weep openly
56 "Not gonna happen!"
57 X-rated
58 Extremely persnickety
60 Maya Angelou poem often read on Juneteenth ... and a hint to this puzzle's theme
62 Doily material
63 Half of an improv comedy duo with Mike Nichols
64 Members of a fraternal order
65 Last-ditch

DOWN

1 Sickly
2 Group of crows
3 Results of coffee spills
4 "... but I could be wrong"
5 Blues singer Thornton who recorded "Hound Dog" before Elvis
6 Redding on Stax Records
7 Unwrap with abandon
8 Elude
9 Refuses to admit
10 Vet's patient
11 Young Greek god?
12 "I wanted to be able to come here and speak with you on this occasion because you are young, gifted, and black" speaker Hansberry
13 Cozy quality
17 Batman, when he's taking a sick day?
21 Make like a frog
24 Animal lower on the food chain
28 Ceremonial first pitch by a celebrity?
30 Bandeaux, e.g.
31 Dart through the air
32 Criterion Collection purchase
34 Non-credit transaction
35 Like extra-credit questions
36 Place for an Apple logo?
38 Currency in Austria
41 Supernatural vibe
43 Look closely at
45 Worked on a manuscript
47 Mid-size Kia
48 Sics on
49 Audience member who isn't moved to tears, metaphorically
52 Submit tax forms online
54 Not as skeptical
57 Freudian mistake
59 Laura of 100 Gecs
61 ___ Vegas

MANE EVENT

BY ANDREW J. RIES

ACROSS

1 Become rotted, perhaps
6 Herb-seasoned pickles
11 "Rumor ___ it ..."
14 Do penance
15 Highly skilled
16 Play a role
17 15-time Argentine Footballer of the Year
19 Radio host Glass
20 Give a "Jeopardy!" response
21 Fires (up)
22 One putting on a front
24 Acquire by freeloading
26 Snail, scallop, or squid
28 Governors J.B. Pritzker and Doug Burgum, for two
31 Lies next to
32 Church headquartered in Salt Lake City: Abbr.
33 Appliance that might be self-cleaning
37 "I like the cut of your ___"
38 Little mischief maker
42 Chopping tool
43 Entry-level title: Abbr.
45 ___ tai (cocktail with a rhyming name)
46 Oprah's production company
48 19th-century Australian coup related to a military-run liquor monopoly
52 "Restaurant Patrons Entranced by Sizzling Order of ___" (headline in The Onion)
55 It's handled in the kitchen
56 Highlight for a Texas tourist
57 Kitty's sound
58 Carpet crawler
61 Tang
62 June celebration ... which is depicted in this puzzle's shaded squares?
66 Actress Longoria
67 Minuscule amounts
68 Black cat of cartoon fame
69 Living room
70 On pins and needles
71 Entertainment center unit

DOWN

1 Fancy affair
2 "Try a Little Tenderness" singer Redding
3 Groups covering many chapters
4 Journalist Curry
5 Iconic Chicago pizza style
6 Add moisture to
7 Mid-month occasion
8 ___ Six (group of composers that included Satie)
9 Vinyl enthusiast's collection
10 Suppress
11 Art form with a 5/7/5 structure
12 Farmland measures
13 Opposite of ornate
18 Brick in a playroom?
23 In addition
25 Part of many musical genre names
26 Skirt style between mini and maxi
27 Words after a guesstimate
28 ___ California (Mexican state)
29 Bird related to the spoonbill
30 Noah's love in "The Notebook"
34 Wines derived from one type of grape
35 Trade show
36 Element #10
39 Title heroine of English literature
40 Metallica drummer Ulrich
41 Sports event featuring ice picks?
44 Quick job for a stylist
47 Everything
49 Perfect world
50 Like John Lee Hooker's music
51 Wyatt of the Old West
52 In a state of confusion
53 Still in the running
54 Country divided into prefectures
57 Smartphones succeeded them: Abbr.
59 Garfield foil
60 Sequence of words
63 Comic White
64 Cousin in "The Addams Family"
65 MLK title

WHERE IT'S AT

BY PATRICK BLINDAUER

ACROSS

1 Hit the road, say
7 Offer from a Nigerian prince, probably
11 Half of 64-Down
14 Writer Jong and violinist Morini
15 Insurance variety
16 Peace, to Caesar
17 What Frankenstein said after tasting his cake ingredients?
19 "Love ___ Battlefield"
20 Place famed for a sparkling wine
21 Inits. on a battleship
22 Skyscraper support
24 Vacation destinations, sometimes
27 Supposed Roswell sighting
28 Something to hold when taking the A train?
34 "The choice of a new generation" sloganeer, once
36 Reed who sang "Walk on the Wild Side"

37 Concert series
38 Family member in NATO's phonetic alphabet
39 Pitch to a customer
41 Swimmer's assignment
42 Viking of fame
43 "Mazel ___!" ("Congratu-lations!")
44 Critic who gave "Police Academy" zero stars
46 Doll for football practice?
49 Place to find a bud
50 Rhode Island city
54 "The Creation" composer
57 Sigma successor
59 Site with bidding wars

60 Yoko of "Double Fantasy"
61 Where the large are in charge?
65 ___ sauce
66 Home of Blarney Castle
67 Is in the debt of
68 Ambient composer of note
69 En route, as a package
70 Cuisine featuring bulgogi

DOWN

1 Prohibit from law practice
2 Take off the TiVo
3 ZaSu of early films
4 Exciting, like "Die Hard"
5 Common middle name

6 Co. that introduced Dungeons & Dragons
7 They may be circular
8 Signals to actors
9 Emulated a food processor
10 Recurring ideas
11 Early role for Ron Howard
12 Houston-based org.
13 Class action
18 Andersen of "Thor and the Amazon Women"
23 Classic soda machine feature
25 Lo-___ graphics
26 Game with a plastic mat
27 Ho's instrument

29 Fruit in some salads
30 "Finding Nemo" eggs
31 Sound of the ocean
32 Selma or Patty, to Maggie
33 Paid intro?
34 Medic or legal starter
35 Massive, as a fail
38 ___ project
40 Popular toy, for short
45 Munich-based manufacturer
47 Jousting weapons
48 Adequate, slangily
51 Like Elvis, at the end
52 Dreaded person?
53 Big name in processed poultry
54 Fire truck feature
55 Unknown auth. credit
56 Chucklehead
57 Do a pirouette
58 Help with a heist
62 Do some fabrication
63 "All good" sign
64 11-Across doubled

NOTHING BUT NET

BY ADESINA O. KOIKI

ACROSS

1 Communicate nonverbally
5 Souk customer, most times
9 "The Lion King" antagonist
13 "Luther" star Elba
15 46-Across's part
16 Commotion
17 A sarcastic comment might get hidden inside of one
18 Beast of burden
19 Album-certifying org.
20 Alternatives to studs
23 Marine mollusks, in debatable fashion
25 A #15 seed defeating a #2 seed in the NCAA Tournament, e.g.
26 Large quantities
30 Mononymous 2000s sitcom starring a country music legend
31 Trouble-free state
32 Econ 101 subject
35 Quickly, quickly
36 Shoe size component
38 Continue tediously

39 Former White House press secretary Psaki
40 Mamba's weapon
41 Scintilla
42 Type of interlaced pattern
46 Person engaged in histrionics
49 Super Bowl LII winners
50 Focused on achieving results
54 "If all ___ fails ..."
55 Persia, today
56 Separates laundry
60 Prone to butting in
61 Mozart's "___ fan tutte"
62 Dance popularized by Chubby Checker
63 1982 Disney cyberfilm with a 2010 sequel

64 Otolaryn-gologists, informally
65 "Negative!"

DOWN

1 [This wasn't my error]
2 Nuptial promise
3 Minions' leader in "Despicable Me"
4 Alcoholic drink taken at bedtime
5 Secret location?
6 Lecherous man
7 ___ breve
8 "Chicken-n-___" (2003 Ludacris album)
9 Long narrow pieces
10 Invents, as a phrase
11 "A friend to all is a friend to none," e.g.

12 Facetious ceremonial tribute
14 Intimidated, in modern slang
21 Poet's "ajar"
22 Highly impolite
23 Like some "The Biggest Loser" contestants, initially
24 Grilled sandwich with ham, pork and Swiss
27 Perch for pigeons
28 Breakfast grain
29 ___ Wednesday
30 Regime opposed by Gandhi
32 Area for fruit trees
33 Goes out with romantically
34 Group with many expert drivers: Abbr.

36 Used to be
37 Tattoos
38 Reduce
40 Card game featuring a banker
42 Last name of Henry VIII's second wife
43 Sport played professionally by transgender pioneer Renée Richards
44 Buddhist monastery
45 Discharge from the body
46 Intelligence employee
47 The "C" in BIPOC
48 Spicy cured pork in Cajun cuisine
51 Private university in Houston
52 Element whose Latin name is "ferrum"
53 It's usually right on the map
57 2016 Summer Olympics site
58 Medicinal or cooking meas.
59 Jeanne d'Arc, par exemple: Abbr.

OUTGROUPS

BY WILL NEDIGER

ACROSS

1 Biggest stars
6 Physicist with a namesake model of the atom
10 Non-main social media accounts, briefly
14 Weezer frontman Rivers
15 Far-jumping insect
16 Fundamental cause
17 *Forever and ever*
19 Basis for Pfizer's Covid-19 vaccine
20 "What's the ___?"
21 *Saturating*
23 Leave alone
25 Entertains
26 Anti-vaping ad, e.g.
29 "To ___, With Love"
30 Like many whistleblowers, briefly
31 Shows on TV
33 Parents' home, metaphorically
35 Abandons at the altar
39 Go from grandparent to grandchild ... or what the answers to this puzzle's italicized clues do?

42 Quick on the uptake
43 Toy grabber in an arcade game
44 Epic tale
45 About 2.5 centimeters
47 Convened
49 "Call Me if You Get Lost" genre
50 Arnold Palmer ingredient, as it's sometimes written
53 Surround on all sides
55 *Self-imposed punishment*
57 Locations for orations
61 Ye ___ Shoppe
62 *Actress on "Good Girls" and "Parks and Recreation"*
64 Company behind J'adore perfume

65 Gherardini family member who modeled for Leonardo da Vinci
66 Tough nut to crack
67 Tools with teeth
68 Substance that flattens a kiss curl
69 Used a needle

DOWN

1 Nailed perfectly
2 Sumptuosity
3 Teensy bit
4 New car highlight
5 British conservatives
6 Undergrad degree for animators
7 Skateboarding trick named for Alan Gelfand
8 Direct

9 Maker of Wayfarer glasses
10 Groups of troops
11 Relative of the lemur
12 A thousand kilos
13 Animals with racks
18 Paying attention to
22 Kenyan village where men aren't allowed to live
24 High-risk type of birth
26 "None for me, thanks"
27 Person surnamed Kaur, probably
28 Rossini composition
30 Not stressed out
32 Warm-weather cocktails
34 NBC staple, familiarly

36 "That's not true!"
37 Men's equivalent of a stola
38 Video that disappears after a short time
40 Condition treated with a CPAP
41 Country where agaseke baskets are made
46 Gondola waterways
48 Headgear with gemstones
50 Touches were the last ones produced
51 Cuban revolutionary Sánchez
52 Provide with funds
53 Soft-drink company mocked on a 1997 Negativland album
54 Nancy, to Fritzi
56 Film class screening
58 Put in the overhead compartment
59 French auxiliary verb
60 Beach towel coating
63 Hider of a bad haircut

SNAP OUT OF IT!

BY ANDREW J. RIES

ACROSS

1 Accord maker
6 Stopped slouching
11 Bit of funny business
14 In regards to
15 Mad as hell
16 "Milk and Honey" artist
17 Ratio in fluid dynamics named for an American scientist
19 Superior of a private: Abbr.
20 Make a note of
21 Prophet who authored the Torah, according to tradition
23 Beef cut from the bottom sirloin
27 River through Juba
28 Does some seamy work?
32 Cause trouble, metaphorically
34 Device with a 2007 debut
36 Prying
37 What a job promotion typically entails
38 Aid in air circulation
39 Auto shop implement
42 100% certain about
44 "Sing it, sister!"
45 University in Winston-Salem, North Carolina
48 "In the Long Run" creator/star Idris
49 Silo weapon: Abbr.
50 Had a videochat with, maybe
52 Cuts back
54 State of immobility
59 Environment-related prefix
60 Reach an agreement ... and what the first words of 17-, 32-, and 45-Across are?

64 City with an annual Carnival
65 Cognizant
66 Volume on a tablet, say
67 "Veep" co-star Richardson
68 State with its own power grid
69 Numbers of a listicle, maybe

DOWN

1 Cause injury to
2 Instrument in the woodwind family
3 Object in a sentence
4 Evidence of disuse
5 Took a loss, informally
6 Kilogram or ampere, e.g.
7 What a sleeve covers
8 Bar bill
9 Sport-___
10 Curly hairstyle
11 TV teen drama with a 2021 sequel series
12 Antagonist in Shakespeare's "Measure for Measure"
13 Became prepared
18 Like the Vikings
22 Unwavering in tone
24 Frequent collaborator of Amy Poehler
25 Laundry room device
26 Hoops scores: Abbr.
28 Title for a knight
29 Organization launched in the Nixon era: Abbr.
30 Handheld cleaner
31 "Yeah, I screwed up. Big deal!"
33 Informal greeting
35 Dart gun brand
38 Tined piece of silverware
40 Fill-in
41 Green ___
43 Goddess of the dawn
44 Dictation-taking pro
45 Pair on a windshield
46 Tree known as a "wattle" in Australia
47 Cruelly treats
51 Discourage
53 Certain jazz singer's specialty
55 Country great McEntire
56 CGI-pioneering film of 1982
57 "Don't worry about me!"
58 Poses a question to
61 "What do I ___ you?"
62 Two-time Formula One world champion Verstappen
63 Stretch of years

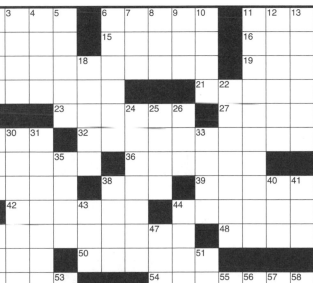

STATE DEPT.

BY PATRICK BLINDAUER

ACROSS

1 Bearded farm creatures
6 Loc. for learning
9 Big aluminum producer
14 Good home for cubists?
15 "I Ching" philosophy
16 Homes for hens
17 Poker pushovers in the Sunshine State?
19 Trim in the Lone Star State?
20 Furniture hardwood
21 Ancient oracle site
23 Six Million Dollar Man's org.
24 Slope rides
26 Elton John musical that's a reimagining of a classical opera
28 Stroll with confidence
31 ___ alai (racquetball cousin)
33 Many a Cecil B. DeMille film
36 Express in words
37 It's quite a trip
38 ___ melt
39 Stun folks in the Mountain State?
41 Having left the Volunteer State?
43 Bar mitzvah dance
44 Goldie of "Laugh-In"
46 Needing nourishment
47 "Out of Africa" author Dinesen
48 Certain Wordsworth work
49 Ridiculously small
50 ___ up (get ready)
52 Cease, at sea
54 What candles may represent
56 Turns way up, as music
58 Remark of realization
62 Bread option in the Gopher State?
64 "Refrain from jeering the Green Mountain State!"?
66 Battleship in 1898 news
67 Firecracker that fizzles
68 Dawning
69 Name on registration document
70 Peter and Paul: Abbr.
71 Last two words of John Lennon's "Imagine"

DOWN

1 Partygoer's purchase
2 Eyeball impolitely
3 Italian carmaker ___ Romeo
4 Excelled, slangily
5 Musical note between "fa" and "la"
6 Take turns?
7 Fast food chain with a star in its logo
8 Institution often named for a saint: Abbr.
9 Second section of "Hamlet"
10 Salty bagel topper
11 Brand with a mascot named Sonny the Cuckoo Bird
12 Latin word for "work"
13 Italian wine center
18 Historic 1944 event
22 Seventeen-syllable poem
25 Give orders like a drill sergeant
27 They make big booms
28 Bar food?
29 Oliver Reed's role in "The Three Musketeers"
30 Place for my stuff or your junk
32 Flux played by Charlize
34 Recon acquisition
35 It might come from Mars
37 Expensive Super Bowl purchase
40 Fingerprint pattern
42 Fat time?: Abbr.
45 Exhaust
49 Sail's support
51 "Li'l ___" (classic comic strip)
53 Does some selling
54 Shooting range supply
55 Chew on persistently
57 Combines, in a way
59 Neither great nor terrible
60 Like some odds, ironically
61 Luncheon extension
63 Dix moins neuf
65 Cabaret accessory

DOUBLE BLOW

BY ADESINA O. KOIKI

ACROSS

1 Belted out
5 "Beowulf," for example
9 Compete à la Team USA Olympian Simone Manuel
13 "Guardians of the Galaxy" hero
15 ___-eaten (old-fashioned)
16 Himalayan legend
17 ___ tatin (upside-down French pastry)
18 Flat-topped hill
19 Course selection?
20 Barney and Betty's son, in cartoondom
23 Earth Day mo.
24 Argument
25 Côte d'Ivoire port city
29 They may be dressed for dinner
33 Sponge (up), as gravy
34 Humpty Dumpty body shape
37 Response after being tagged, perhaps
38 2015 International Boxing Hall of Fame inductee whose given first name is Ray
42 "The West Wing" actor Alan
43 Afro–Puerto Rican musical style
44 Animated frame
45 Wiped away, as one's hopes
48 Suffer humiliation
50 Falstaffian in appearance
53 California's Big ___
54 Fried seafood dish covered in Thai sweet chili sauce
60 Patent precursor
61 Muscles targeted by a dead bug (wait ... what?!)
62 Be of assistance to
64 Not now
65 Beehive State city that's an anagram of a world capital
66 Pigeon's urban perch
67 Swirling current
68 ___ pot (nasal cavity rinser)
69 Platform for tweets?

DOWN

1 Boot camp VIP
2 The "A" of UAE
3 "Awkwafina Is ___ From Queens"
4 Became heated, in a sense
5 Oscar winner Stone or Thompson
6 Amanda Gorman works
7 Informal identification
8 Nautical maps
9 Representative
10 ___ Ewbank, head coach of the Super Bowl III–winning New York Jets
11 Type for stressing: Abbr.
12 ⅟₅₀₀ of the Indianapolis 500
14 Gig from an employment agency
21 "Watch What Happens Live With Andy Cohen" network
22 The Jazz, in box scores
25 Equally crappy
26 Yalie's cheer word
27 Nano and Shuffle, for two
28 Gaming rookie
30 Italian's friends
31 Rob's Place, in the 1970s sitcom "What's Happening!!"
32 Wilt the ___ (a nickname of NBA great Chamberlain)
35 Text's "If you ask me ..."
36 "Let's continue this online convo in private"
39 Reddish-brown color
40 Embarrass
41 Person with inborn talent
46 Flow's tidal opposite
47 Demon ___ (Wake Forest University athlete)
49 Motivated
51 One way to keep a mate awake in the bedroom
52 White-plumed wading bird
54 Vampire's attack
55 Ritalin treats it: Abbr.
56 One may be crying
57 What comes immediately after a quarter
58 Neat, like a bed
59 Truffle finders
63 Tennis redo

GETTING WARMER

BY WILL NEDIGER

ACROSS

1 ___ Romeo
5 Full of ripples
9 Subject for a grammarian or a fashionista
14 Like the first sauce on "Hot Ones"
15 People who've moved on, maybe
16 Currently winning
17 *Subtitle of the second "To All the Boys" film*
20 November/December zodiac sign, casually
21 ___ O's
22 Body parts you might boop
23 "___ you do that??"
25 Wombs
27 *Creator of Mary Poppins*
30 Ore smelting waste material
34 He played Grandpa on "The Munsters"
35 Pampering, briefly
38 Enfant terrible?
39 "Wi' ___ Wee Bairn Ye'll Me Beget" (song by the Magnetic Fields)
40 Alphabetical (order)
41 Cartoonist Chast
42 Pros who might get sacked
43 AOL exchanges
44 Vote in favor
45 Generally speaking
47 Structure with paredes
49 *Sleepovers*
51 Architect who lived to 102
54 Bent the truth
55 Painful struggle
57 Bread that's often seasoned with garlic
59 Hair streak substance
62 Mathematical task done increasingly accurately by the beginnings of the answers to the italicized clues?
65 "Ciao!"
66 "White Flag" singer
67 Make (your way)
68 Geeklike
69 Guesses by 33-Down
70 Redding on Stax

DOWN

1 Sound boosters
2 Frank whose designs were featured on many Trapper Keepers
3 Like penguins and ostriches
4 Sponsored content, essentially
5 Uncomfortable feeling
6 Rotating shaft
7 Velvety fabric
8 Major monogram in fashion
9 Sip on, perhaps
10 Many a senior project
11 Pop genre for France Gall and Françoise Hardy
12 Socialist country in Southeast Asia
13 upenn.___
18 ___ zone (risky place to park)
19 1
24 Unrefined rock
26 Sandal variety
27 Stock market crisis
28 Alpaca relative
29 Much-needed holiday
31 Intake after oral surgery, often
32 Stroll casually
33 Navigation devices
36 Manhattan Project town
37 Russian empress
46 Road map abbr.
48 Easily-lost earbud
50 Celebrate too early, maybe
52 One of Peter Rabbit's sisters
53 According to
55 Effect of the Moon's gravity
56 Razor target
58 Opera set in the Old Kingdom
60 Symbol of life-giving energy, in Hinduism
61 Comes to a close
62 Attracted to all genders
63 Palin___ (poem that retracts an earlier poem)
64 19-Down doubled

FLYING COLORS

BY ANDREW J. RIES

ACROSS

1 Temporarily give
5 After that
9 Egyptian snakes
13 "To clarify ..."
15 Soccer great Wambach
16 "In Living Color" segment
17 *Another name for a half bath*
19 One may have an extra letter
20 Male buds
21 Film protagonist Emmet Brickowski and others
23 It's a blast in the comics
26 Metaphorical drink for a harsh critic
27 Slightly
28 Unit of electrical current, for short
30 Mix with a spoon
31 Knocks over
32 Johnson Space Center org.
34 Poles on a ship's deck
37 Even one
38 *Monarch's "I"*
40 Song that charts well
41 Musical pace
43 Car, van, or truck
44 Section of a window
45 "Aha, now I see"
47 Sound like a pigeon
48 Kurylenko of "Black Widow"
49 Lickety-split
52 Gave shelter to
54 "I can work with that"
55 Precisely
56 Actor/singer Jared
57 Company with an initial launch in July 2021 ... and a feature of the italicized clues' answers?
62 Cosmetics giant
63 Got up
64 Kind of drum
65 Roman equivalent of the Greek war god Ares
66 "Author unknown" notation: Abbr.
67 Visually assessed

DOWN

1 Target for some gloss
2 Musical offshoot of punk
3 Just released
4 Pop physiques, say
5 Puts blacktop on
6 Name dropped from Max
7 Tributary of the Congo River
8 MLB All-Star Pete Alonso's team
9 Queens neighborhood that borders Sunnyside
10 *Plane safety officials*
11 Played a fife, perhaps
12 Mancala game piece
14 Emperor after Claudius
18 Cheese often combined with Parmesan
22 "You understand?"
23 Unit of gold's fineness
24 Do penance
25 *Device in a crib*
26 British condiment that's like a brown ketchup
29 "I Shall Not Be Moved" poet Angelou
33 Choir singer's range
35 Flash of color
36 Place
38 1976 novel subtitled "The Saga of an American Family"
39 "Yippee!"
42 Electromagnetic particles theorized by Einstein
44 Fries/cheese curds/gravy dish
46 Singer featured on Gotye's "Somebody That I Used to Know"
49 The world's second-largest religion
50 3-Down, in Spanish
51 Cantaloupe, for one
53 Canoe propellers
55 One between 12 and 20
58 Base entertainment group: Abbr.
59 Like many "Pose" characters
60 Anger
61 Connecticut governor Lamont

DOUBLE FEATURES

BY PATRICK BLINDAUER

ACROSS
1 Part of a place setting
6 Word before Major or Minor
10 "___ in Show"
14 "Easy, baby!"
15 Get better
16 Cookie in which my kid replaced the creme with cheese and tried to get me to eat it
17 Outdo by a bit
18 Group with many boomers
19 ___ vision
20 2009 film about illegal street racing
23 Pioneer in instant messaging
24 Old photograph tint
28 Reach for the Skyy, for example
32 Candidates for excommunication
35 "The Last Supper," for one
36 What Brits call beans in veggie burgers
37 Old-fashioned contraction
38 2005 film based on a Jane Austen novel
42 NYPD alert
43 Many moons
44 They can be slipped on
45 Reaction seekers
48 Trick-taking card game
49 Owner of Jimmy Dean and Hillshire Farm
50 Had some sole, say
51 1997 film with George Clooney in one of the title roles
59 "No ___!"
62 Knitting shop purchase
63 Picked
64 Improve, as a skill
65 Elton's "Don't Go Breaking My Heart" duet partner
66 "___ the Lilacs" (Louisa May Alcott novel)
67 Boardwalk or Park Place card
68 Threat-ending word
69 ___ with (teased)

DOWN
1 Plum, for one, briefly
2 "Stormy Weather" singer Horne
3 Brewery offerings
4 Stretched tight
5 Contractable's opposite
6 Rental company since 1945
7 "___ Window" (Hitchcock film)
8 Wrap at an Indian restaurant, perhaps
9 Brand once pitched by Garfield
10 Complete works, maybe
11 Mess up
12 Parting subject for Moses
13 Item in a Happy Meal
21 Rival
22 Cause of wear and tear
25 Felt compassion for
26 Spike in freezing weather?
27 Put a value on
28 "Brace for ___!"
29 Eddie who voiced Donkey in "Shrek"
30 Unethical payments
31 Alternative to DCA or BWI
32 Some are English and some are French
33 "Keep your ___ peeled"
34 Bollywood legend Kapoor
36 Leopard feature
39 South American mountain range
40 Knockout punch, at times
41 Traffic control?: Abbr.
46 Descended on
47 Words before jam or pickle
48 Get to one's feet
50 "It's the Hard Knock Life" musical
52 Big Wheel rider
53 Pony Express concern
54 Boats like Noah's
55 "How dreadful!"
56 Factor in a wine review
57 "Duly noted"
58 Eugene in "Grease," for example
59 Pres. Wilson held one
60 Notable plaintiff of 1973
61 "Ready Player ___"

ON/OFF THE CLOCK

BY ADESINA O. KOIKI

ACROSS

1 Monogram of a '60s Attorney General
4 Thirst ___ (provocative selfie)
8 Electronic echo
14 Fútbol cheer
15 Genesis name?
16 Wonder at the piano
17 Personnel hired and paid in quotidian fashion
19 Five Nations tribe
20 Handmade-crafts site
21 Identifies, in a way
23 Verve
24 Apt name for a Dalmatian
26 "Okay, that makes sense"
29 With 47-Across, facetious question to someone putting in a shift
34 Look of satisfaction
36 "Hot ___" (YouTube series involving celebrities eating chicken wings)
37 Words before roll or whim
38 Stood in the shadows
39 "I dunno"
42 Far from affable
43 Popular bandage brand
44 Iowa State University city
45 Sommelier's selections
47 See 29-Across
51 School where Jackie Robinson lettered in four sports: Abbr.
52 Isn't wrong?
53 Jheri curl, e.g.
56 Pharaoh's resting place
58 "I'm all ___!"
62 Gets accustomed (to)
65 Symbolic end of summer

67 Defensive specialist in volleyball
68 Way to sit by
69 Incomplete status, as in an auto race: Abbr.
70 Did some sowing
71 Highland refusals
72 Proverbial limit

DOWN

1 Traveled by horseback
2 Heelless shoe
3 Alicia who is a wonder at the piano
4 LAX screeners
5 Schedule for another date
6 Rodent related to the guinea pig
7 Haircut line
8 ___ feed
9 Summer, on the Côte d'Azur
10 Facade
11 Stunt legend Knievel
12 Costa ___
13 Noggin
18 Mr. Clean rival
22 Communicates nonverbally
25 High school math class, informally
27 ___ butter (lotion ingredient)
28 Rout
29 More expansive
30 "Au contraire!"
31 Washing, as dishes
32 Formerly
33 Many catch them on the beach
34 Former monarch of Iran

35 Mineral found in granite
40 ___ nitrite (blood vessel dilator)
41 Still learning, perhaps
46 Sect or net lead-in
48 On the receiving end of a Dear John letter
49 Holiday Inn rival
50 Pet food component
53 Amigos
54 Falco of "The Sopranos"
55 Broccoli ___ (salad green)
57 Actress Lena of "Alias"
59 Performs some arithmetic
60 High social position
61 "Sharknado" cable channel
63 "Boyz n the Hood" protagonist
64 Lawn repair supply
66 Kvetching cries

FREE JAZZ

BY WILL NEDIGER

ACROSS

1 "Wanna hear a secret?"
5 Number of letters in the title of any Juan Filloy novel
10 Daddy, in Spanish
14 Salt Lake City's state
15 Kimberly who played Denver in "Beloved"
16 Parsons with a "project"
17 It might be required to get a tattoo
20 New York city named after an ancient Tunisian city
21 Seed in a pod
22 Piano student's piece
23 Thrift store stipulation
25 Like the "y" sound in "yam"
27 "You'll have to remind me"
31 Longtime rulers of Italy
32 Cake made with lentils and rice
33 Bliss
36 Use an inkjet
37 "___ you kidding me?"
38 Gradually destroy
40 Pathetic
41 Game company that released "Fortnite"
43 Aviator Earhart
44 Sense of right and wrong
46 Word a surgeon might say while holding out a hand
50 Site of some accords criticized by Edward Said
51 Snowboarding trick
52 Certain hosp. area
54 "___ sera" (Italian "good evening")
58 Harmonic progression heard on albums like "Giant Steps" ... or a hint to the shaded letters

DOWN

1 ___ platter
2 "Right now!"
3 Draupadi wears one that magically extends itself, in the "Mahabharata"
4 Most-highly valued literary works, collectively
5 Group
6 Go by, as time
7 Apt anagram of "evil"
8 Daring adventure
9 Opposite of "paleo-"
10 Good food for carbo-loading
11 Indigenous Alaskan
12 One of the animal mascots of the '08 Beijing Olympics
13 Info gathered by a spy
18 Tendency to get really mad
19 Soprano with an eponymous peach dessert
24 American equivalent of Canada's CRA
26 Completely
27 Wi-Fi suppliers
28 Swimmer Torres who won medals in five different Olympics
29 "Metamorphoses" poet
30 Approximately
33 Serious shock
34 Cartoon dog originally named Spot
35 Number you might type into a time machine
37 Part of Delta's fleet
39 Formally give up
42 "The Raven" author
43 Cooling units, briefly
45 Appealingly sordid
46 They're sometimes worn with sandals
47 Sound of a mic drop
48 Place for strikes and spares
49 About a kilogram of water
53 "Finally" singer Peniston
55 Monstrous creature
56 "The Day the Earth Stood Still" co-star Patricia
57 Long slitherers
59 Yodeler's site
60 One prone to brooding

61 Patella's place
62 Queso ingredient
63 "Darn!"
64 Yogurt-like food from Iceland
65 Fuss over appearances
66 Long swimmers

BROKEN CLOCK

BY Andrew J. Ries

ACROSS

1 Occasion for a swim team
5 Relating to a certain geometric shape
10 The ___ (pic site)
14 ___ mater
15 Spin, as a baton
16 Louisiana's largest city, informally
17 Portrayer of Parker in "The Social Network"
19 Country on the Persian Gulf
20 Seat at a rodeo
21 Devices that finely chop potatoes
23 Stuff from a pump
24 Servers claim it
27 Div. for the Oakland A's
30 Hebrew name that's an anagram of "Chaim"
31 Meadows
32 Duel opponent of Hector in the "Iliad"
34 Completely spent
38 Not close
39 Deadlocked contest
41 Unit of light or hope
42 Strong passion
44 Lose stamina
45 Something that's struck by a model
46 "A Theory of Justice" philosopher John
48 Formally accepts
50 Popular podcast genre
54 Tolkien brute
55 Kind of cord used by a daredevil
56 1997 Jonny Lang song whose title is a request for untruths
60 Samoa's capital
61 Windows of opportunity ... and a feature of this puzzle's theme answers?
64 Soul singer Bridges
65 Shoes with holes
66 Struggle with sibilants
67 Late-night host who won the Mark Twain Prize in 2014
68 Couldn't back out
69 All-in-one printer function

DOWN

1 STEM field, for short
2 Kazan of Hollywood history
3 Honor for a showrunner
4 Cats with many stripes
5 ___-Alt-Del
6 Small head-turner
7 DaCosta who directed 2021's "Candyman"
8 Annoy
9 Non-secular worker
10 Dumplings often made with potatoes
11 See 27-Down
12 Basic smartphone app
13 Majestic dwelling
18 Some units at farmers' markets
22 Blown away
25 Literary movement for Amy Lowell
26 Movie studio whose mascot is a desk lamp
27 With 11-Down, Italian sports carmaker
28 Play king
29 ___ chi
33 Beijing-born action movie star
35 Performer using objects in their act
36 What E can stand for
37 Coloring substances
39 Vestigal amount
40 ___ culpa
43 Shakerful at a pizzeria
45 Doorways in much science fiction
47 Pejorative sung in "Amazing Grace"
49 Person who's very active
50 Game with little hitters
51 Indian bread?
52 Industry group
53 Verb on many campaign signs
57 "In that case ..."
58 ___ Verde (national park in Colorado)
59 "Around the Horn" channel
62 Glass or Glasser
63 Unauthorized video game tweak

DOWNCAST

BY PATRICK BLINDAUER

ACROSS

1 Prepares for showing, as a house
7 "___ Little Teapot"
10 Form of Spanish "to be"
14 Chuck E. Cheese attraction
15 Home of the Stern School of Business: Abbr.
16 Hurt badly
17 Successful swinger
18 Quesadilla component
20 Things cast from far away
22 ___ Speedwagon
23 Mo. with Aries and Taurus births
24 They may be stolen while people stand there and watch
25 Legend creator
28 German interjection
30 PhD program prerequisite, often
31 Company that brought Space Invaders into the home
33 Curse word?
35 Cause for a child's punishment, perhaps

36 Like some rhythms
39 Cabinet member: Abbr.
42 Male delivery?
43 Spills, as from a bucket
46 Prefix with friendly or logical
47 "Singin' in the Rain" studio
49 Is right next to
51 Like some suckers
55 Brand of lip balm
57 Item in a caddie's bag
58 Captain Kirk's kissing partner in "Plato's Stepchildren"
62 Site of experimentation on a station in orbit

63 Place of pure perfection
64 Org. in charge of food stamps?
65 "The ___ Club" (1970s–80s TV show)
66 Seaport southeast of Roma
67 Bug bomb victim
68 Call, in poker
69 Black eye, slangily

DOWN

1 It means "desert" in Arabic
2 Manhattan area next to Chinatown
3 Causes a classroom disturbance, perhaps
4 Place for a plane to park

5 Plot of Genesis?
6 Mattress maker based near Atlanta
7 Easily swapped out
8 "Butt out," briefly
9 Pervasive atmospheres
10 Hirsch of "Into the Wild"
11 Lea who won a Tony for "Miss Saigon"
12 Joust participants
13 Builds, as a fortune
19 "Trading Spaces" channel
21 Pollution watchdog org.
26 Slightly shocking
27 Melber of MSNBC

29 John Denver's "I Guess ___ Rather Be in Colorado"
32 Org. authorized by the 16th Amendment
34 Greek letters after nus
35 Pretentious person
37 Internet address ending
38 ___ carte (menu phrase)
39 Closes completely
40 Third book in the "Twilight" series
41 They share top billing
44 Taken advantage of
45 Free from germs
48 Calendar column abbr.
50 Invigorating feature of the oceanside
52 Former coin of Austria
53 Picked at some lox, say
54 Barks like a Chihuahua
56 Flabbergasts
59 Silver of sabermetrics
60 State with six sides
61 Arizona natives

HOUSE EXPANSION

BY ADESINA O. KOIKI

ACROSS

1 One of a deadly septet
4 Consider again, with "at"
10 "Lifestyles of the ___ and Famous"
14 Tumult
15 Geronimo or Cochise, tribally
16 Petro-Canada rival
17 Hauled ass, say
18 Like some alternative approaches to medicine
20 Melville's obsessed captain
22 Legal contract between an employer and a union: Abbr.
23 Hex broken in half?
24 Something commonly used by a punster
27 Followed a curve
31 Onetime twosomes
32 "Lady Marmalade" group (1974) or its lead singer
34 "Light" sci-fi weapon
36 Diwali wrap
38 Be in the red
39 Not based on repeated sections or verses, in music
43 Suffix denoting tumors
44 Straightforward
45 Loosely compacted sediment
46 Person whom "Karens" frequently want to speak to
49 "Dem ___" (affectionate nickname for the bygone Brooklyn Dodgers)
50 Confuse
51 Capital of Cambodia
56 Student advocacy gp.
58 It's "understood" in certain sentences
59 Superfood berry
60 Last part of a race ... and what 24-, 39-, and 51-Across do to some letters contained in 18-Across?
65 66-Across's opposite
66 65-Across's opposite
67 Envelope or folder option
68 Word following a married name, perhaps
69 Indian musical pattern
70 Declared
71 ICU attendants: Abbr.

DOWN

1 New York's ___ Lawrence College
2 Pocatello locale
3 Discount shopper's purchase
4 "Yay team!"
5 Geologic divisions of time
6 Sporty Italian auto, for short
7 ___ Spray (juice brand commonly used in mixed drinks on college campuses)
8 Expression of mock surprise
9 Held onto
10 Abandon, as a tennis match
11 "To some extent" suffix
12 CBS crime drama franchise
13 Ad ___ committee
19 Many a Middle East resident
21 The "sweet science," en español
25 The Incas' modern-day home
26 One of the Jetsons
28 Well-performing runner-up
29 Actor Cary
30 Titles to property
33 Axe-thrower's skill
34 Opening in a leaf
35 Arabic name meaning "highly praised"
36 Cheddar cheese descriptor
37 Summertime coolers, for short
40 "___ whiz!"
41 Kelsey ___, WNBA star and all-time leading scorer in NCAA women's basketball
42 Start of a "Willy Wonka & the Chocolate Factory" song
47 Michigan city on Lake Huron
48 Understands, colloquially
49 Looped yarn
52 Doglike African scavenger
53 Part of the majority, in a game of tag
54 Auto safety advocate Ralph
55 Conceals
57 Devices requiring PINs
60 "Fight for You" singer (2021)
61 Eggs in a fertility lab
62 Novelist Wolitzer
63 Snitch
64 Possessed

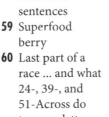

CAN'T LOSE

BY WILL NEDIGER

ACROSS

1 Devices with circular mirrors, often
5 Kick out of office
9 Flirt with, maybe
14 "Curses!"
15 Counterpart of pizzicato
16 ___ on the side of caution
17 Self-important question
20 Get the ball rolling
21 Not in stock quite yet
22 Make into law
25 Wu-Tang Clan member, casually
26 "I've gotten my comeuppance"
30 Flash drive letters
33 Startled greeting
34 Former horse girl?
35 ___ beauty
37 Cries of distress
39 Creamy trattoria dish
41 Activated, as an alarm system
42 Brand originally called Froffles
44 Relatives with sobrinos
45 "Mudbound" director Rees
46 "Christina's World" painter
49 Polarizing type of beer
50 "A Bell for ___" (John Hersey novel)
51 Stage coverer
54 Wild donkey
58 Scenario that works out for everyone ... or a hint to this puzzle's theme
61 Have leftovers, maybe
62 Straddling
63 "My treat"
64 Surname of three influential Chinese sisters
65 Trees with poisonous leaves
66 Poems of homage

DOWN

1 Checks whether a magic square works
2 Gait slower than a canter
3 Civilization that built Tikal
4 Like a sale that covers every aisle
5 Grown-up acorn
6 Diner vessel
7 Bird or Lime vehicle
8 It might have a central square
9 People from Iran's capital
10 Gradually break down
11 "Testimony: Vol. 1" and "Testimony: Vol. 2" singer India
12 Verb in a steak recipe
13 Genre for many DJs
18 Magazine name that rhymes with "chutney"
19 Sported
23 Word for BTS's fan base
24 Came to a close
26 Wanderer
27 Hyatt Regency ___ Chicago (hotel near an airport)
28 "What did I do to deserve this?"
29 Bordered (on)
30 ___ the knot (get divorced)
31 Programmed to
32 Allie who created the webcomic "Hyperbole and a Half"
36 "Am I the only reasonable person here?"
38 Turning into a musical, e.g.
40 State where several Marilynne Robinson novels take place
43 Countertop option
47 Alternative to roti
48 League that celebrated its 25th anniversary in 2021
49 "Crocodile Hunter" Steve
51 "Bye!"
52 A law ___ itself
53 "Dearie me!"
55 Cheese covering
56 City built on seven hills
57 Tenths of a tenner
58 Nickname that omits "ley"
59 Rescue, as a stranded driver
60 Company with brown vehicles

THE SILENCE OF THE LAMBS

BY ANDREW J. RIES

ACROSS

1 50%
5 Neighbor of Burkina Faso
10 Really surprise
14 Most-populous continent
15 Rodgers who guest-hosted "Jeopardy!" in 2021
16 Crazy, in Spanish
17 *Bit of dialogue about a Brit's belly?*
19 Not doing anything
20 Genetically receive
21 Self-destructive soccer gaffe
23 Casual shirt
24 Fortune teller
26 Sports org. that includes the Tucson Roadrunners
27 *Majority of a truck driver's hours?*
32 Crime in some insurance scams
35 Dark drink
36 Member of the fam
37 With a godlike quality
38 Deceptive moves
40 Letters that start many addresses
41 Mahershala of "Ramy"
42 Letting in a breeze, as a room
43 Short-tempered
44 *One harshly criticizing an insult?*
48 Reeeeeeally long time
49 Word after pumping or curling
50 ___ tai
53 "Easy peasy!"
57 Game with an unmatchable card
59 Honorific title in the Ottoman Empire
60 *Footwear worn by a stinging insect?*
62 Video game–inspired Disney franchise
63 Bracelet closer
64 Region
65 Uses needle and thread
66 Supports on a bed frame
67 Broadway performer's prize

DOWN

1 Something that can be kicked
2 In unison
3 Limber
4 Destined outcome
5 Of lesser quality, as meat
6 Top with neck straps
7 Comic Shaffir
8 Off-limits action
9 From the top
10 Disparaging remark
11 Errand runners' references
12 Sch. that owns the Geffen Playhouse
13 French for "Christmas"
18 "The Trial" director Welles
22 Zip
25 1979 blockbuster that's a sequel to a Best Picture winner
27 ___ George
28 Blue state?
29 Golfer nicknamed "the Big Easy"
30 Baker's protector
31 Best Athlete, for one
32 Literary character with a leg made of whalebone
33 Candy in a tube-shaped package
34 Presentation with still imagery
38 Cube with dots
39 Flub
40 "I Can't Breathe" Grammy winner
42 Cream-treated condition
43 Watches over
45 Ames dames and such
46 "Survivor" host Jeff
47 Aquatic animals with tentacles
50 Intro to economics?
51 Pulitzer-winning poet Conrad ___
52 "And how!"
53 Divisional rival of the Phils
54 Fairy tale beast
55 Letters that can be derived from "basics," aptly
56 Bridge-crossing fee
58 Installation of castle security
61 Lamb's sound ... which must be "silenced" to make sense of the italicized clues' answers

THAT SOUNDS SPOOOOKY!

BY PATRICK BLINDAUER

ACROSS

1 Bread box, say
4 Furry sci-fi creatures
9 Off the mark
14 Garment patented by Christine Hardt in 1889
15 ___ silence
16 "Divine Comedy" poet
17 Spooky sound from a baseball catcher?
19 Support, as a college
20 Done with
21 Battle of Hastings locale
23 Dominate, informally
24 Add up again
26 "___ Flux" (2005 Charlize Theron movie)
28 Spooky sound from former "Family Feud" host Richard?
33 So, You've Been ___ (board game)
36 Capital of Zambia?
37 Port city of Norway
38 Excellent tennis serve
39 Some urban expansions
43 Little rapscallion
44 Bit of thunder
46 That WNBA player
47 Cause to be embarrassed
49 Spooky sound from Quasimodo?
53 Gets a glimpse of
54 Kidnaps, as aliens supposedly do
58 Member of a sales force
60 Neighbor of Idaho
63 "A Streetcar Named Desire" director Kazan
64 Go ___ (cooperate)
66 Spooky sound from rapper/actor Cube?
68 Kinda
69 Used a crowbar on
70 Wrist-shoulder connector
71 Brief but meaningful
72 ___ packing (fires)
73 Walston of "My Favorite Martian" or Bradbury who wrote "The Martian Chronicles"

DOWN

1 Detest
2 Store of valuable things
3 "American Buffalo" playwright David
4 Fraction of a joule
5 Marie Curie's birthplace
6 Non-alcoholic beer brand
7 South Korean autos
8 Shem and Ham, to Noah
9 Madison Avenue VIP
10 "The soft-minded ___ always fears change": Martin Luther King Jr.
11 Jakarta's country
12 Pack, as luggage into an overhead bin
13 In stitches?
18 Slowly crumble
22 Flip chart supporter
25 Surfers have them, usually
27 Spanish for "gold"
29 Netflix drama starring Bateman and Linney
30 "The Emperor's ___ Groove" (Disney film)
31 "___ for the poor"
32 Hebrew letter before resh
33 "Into ___ life some rain must fall": Longfellow
34 Rights-defending gp.
35 Baseball or football, for example
40 Something to grow out of
41 ___ room (play area)
42 "Because I ___ so!"
45 Gear such as N95 masks: Abbr.
48 More melancholy
50 Icy Hot competitor
51 Start with enthusiasm
52 Took down a peg
55 Like good explanations
56 Wonder Woman's headpiece
57 Pal of Frank and Dean
58 Coarse file
59 "The Time Machine" race
61 Pass receivers?
62 Farmland fraction
65 To the ___ degree
67 Media that newer computers can't read

YOU'RE STARTING TO SCARE ME AGAIN!

BY ADESINA O. KOIKI

ACROSS

1 Pleasant refuge
6 Responded in court
10 Beginning of an apology
13 Kelly with the 1998 album "Soul of a Woman"
14 Still in the tournament
15 Guns N' Roses' Rose
16 Fay Wray or Jamie Lee Curtis, to movie buffs
18 Chop with an axe
19 Not relaxed
20 "Star Trek" android
21 Oscar winner for her role in "Moonstruck"
25 Member of USA's 2008 Ryder Cup–winning team who went undefeated (2-0-1)
29 Oxygen-consuming bacteria
31 Fills with love
32 Experimental action
33 Short response to a long post
34 "Saved by the Bell" character who helps Zack Morris with his homework
40 Chips ___!
41 Eagerly enjoyed
43 Finch in "To Kill a Mockingbird"
47 Record of an affair?
49 Rapid weight-loss options
51 Professor's specialty
52 Complain
53 Ivory/Coast setting
55 Purge
56 Environment where confirmation bias breeds
63 Team outfit, for short
64 Mishit, as a golf ball or a field goal
65 Choppy
66 Ending for host or baron
67 "Too bad" feeling
68 Affectionate term for a boxer

DOWN

1 Military activities, briefly
2 Quadratic function shape
3 Title for longtime Manchester United coach Alex Ferguson
4 "Rocks"
5 Principal location
6 Former planet reclassified in 2006
7 Fraudulent account?
8 She played Brianna on ABC's "Queens"
9 Wild animal's abode
10 Response after receiving a lei
11 New Hampshire town with a prep school
12 Without exceptions
14 Sharp flat-screen TV brand
17 Pearl used in earrings
20 Length equal to 10 meters: Abbr.
21 Sylvester of Looney Tunes, e.g.
22 Belonging to that queen
23 Congressman Swalwell
24 One may be heard on safari
26 "Alas," in modern lingo
27 Prefix with sperm
28 Q-tips' target
30 What you shouldn't mix colors with (unless you like tie-dye)
33 Shakespeare's "your"
35 Former Israeli prime minister Barak
36 Panera competitor
37 James or Jones of jazz
38 Keister
39 Apartment overseer, informally
42 Shade of green
43 Collect gradually
44 Prepares for the Berlin Marathon, say
45 "Doctor Who" time machine
46 Co. affected by net neutrality
47 Pancake house order
48 Book of the Bible that contains the story of Purim: Abbr.
50 Magazine with a Power 100 list
54 Not a piece of cake
56 Second sight ability, for short
57 One half of a Christogram symbol
58 Panama, for example
59 Bovine sound
60 Illness
61 IVF donation
62 Other half of a Christogram symbol

I KNOW THIS ONE!

BY WILL NEDIGER

ACROSS

1 Deep blue something
4 Chewing your nails, e.g.
9 Accumulate, as a tab
14 Belonging to that guy
15 Scottish singer Sandé
16 "Power" star Hardwick
17 "This is terrible"
18 Hesitant answer to the question "The film 'American Gigolo' features what Blondie song?"
20 With 53-Across, hesitant answer to the question "Who starred with M. Ryan in 'Sleepless in Seattle'?"
22 Sweetie
23 Maple tree substance
24 "This meme is so relatable"
25 Having more wisdom to dispense
28 Common first name in both Czech and Japanese
29 Network that aired "Gilmore Girls"
31 Neither's partner
32 Contribute, as to an account
33 Not willing to budge on
35 Guiding principles
36 Confident answer to the question "What early 2000s show is about three sisters who are witches?"
39 Units of pumpernickel
40 Red wall component
41 Not yet satisfied
42 Comedian Edebiri
43 Kurosawa film whose name means "to live"
47 Franchise with a Hawai'i spinoff
48 Spice mixture
50 Arabian Peninsula port
51 Opposite of nothing
52 Nothing
53 See 20-Across
55 Confident answer to the question "How do you say 'goal' in French?"
59 Rank in go or judo
60 Take home from the shelter
61 Moment
62 Texted "If you ask me ..."
63 Lives in temporarily
64 Headgear like a hairnet
65 Bau cua tôm cá holiday

DOWN

1 "Be quiet!"
2 Like Neptune, in the list of planets
3 Really too bad
4 "Shucks" cousin
5 Collect
6 "The Fresh Prince of ___-Air"
7 Not feeling well
8 Lumberjack's cry
9 Vatican City's city
10 Thurman of "Dangerous Liaisons"
11 Outspoken detractor
12 City dweller
13 Containers for cobblers
19 Body part tugged during a game of charades
21 Ahead-of-the-curve artistic movements
26 Poker payment
27 "Farewell!"
28 Dreidel holiday
30 Stereotypical artist's hat
32 "Casino" actor Joe
34 You might slide into them
35 "Okay, I've heard enough"
36 Come to a close
37 Musical mocked in "The Haunting of Lin-Manuel Miranda"
38 Skillet metal
39 Nutritional snack with a moon in its logo
42 Divvies up
44 "Go me!"
45 Give a different title
46 Disentangle
48 It bought (and later sold) the Waterman Pen Company
49 Genre with four-on-the-floor beats
52 Blockchain purchases, briefly
54 Annoyed, with "off"
56 Make a decision
57 Vase with a pedestal
58 Rivière, across the Pyrenees

SERVICE CENTER

BY ANDREW J. RIES

ACROSS

1 Alphabetic knowledge
5 Brand with many foam products
9 Structure at a shipping port
14 Capital of Qatar
15 Erlenmeyer who invented the Erlenmeyer flask
16 Goosebumps-inducing
17 When many popular radio shows are aired
19 Musical genre for Rubén Blades
20 Made of a certain citrus
21 Accoutrements
23 What you eat
24 Parapsychologist's study
25 Unit of corn
27 Owl's claw
29 Romantic drama with three players
33 Goal of some puzzle-solving teams
36 General, for one
37 Teeny bit
38 The world of theater, emblematically
39 Small drink

40 Tree with dark wood
42 Yellow-brown color
43 Head holder
45 Media player originally called SoundJam
46 Not engaged in a heated debate
49 SoFi Stadium athlete, briefly
50 Volcanic eruption emission
51 Toy dog's sound
54 Look over
56 Go sky high
58 "___ Wilds" (sci-fi video game)
60 Big-headed golf clubs
62 Its branches symbolize peace
64 Font similar to Helvetica

65 Region
66 Suffers from pain
67 "Pimp Juice" rapper
68 Coup d'___ (government overthrow)
69 Meat-and-potatoes dish

DOWN

1 Confuse
2 He replaced Theresa as British prime minister
3 Enos of NASA history, e.g.
4 Ctrl + S action
5 Fishing boat item
6 One who's left home
7 Coat of ice
8 Device that snares pet-bothering pests

9 Anderson who directed "The French Dispatch"
10 In a direct fashion
11 Virginia site of a military cemetery
12 Get out of bed
13 Impressive accomplishment
18 Morning shot of espresso, maybe
22 Hiking hazard
26 Blvd. crosser
28 Landmark that's the second-deepest of its kind in the U.S.
29 Stay (behind)
30 A tot might pedal one
31 Area bounded by a dotted line
32 Ice cream brand with a Slow Churned line

33 Is, in Spanish
34 Random guess
35 Fat with a high smoke point
39 Word derived from the Yiddish for "talk"
41 Accept as fact
44 Listings on a terminal display: Abbr.
45 Org. impersonated in some phone scams
47 Damaging individual
48 Creamy breakfast fare
51 Chambers of the heart
52 Staggers
53 Opposite of "rotten"
54 Goose relative
55 Apple junk
57 Tons and tons
59 Home for many Mormons
61 Like a fox
63 November honoree who can be found in the middle of 17-, 29-, 46-, and 62-Across

PAST, PRESENT, AND FUTURE

BY PATRICK BLINDAUER

ACROSS

1 Editorial "let it stand"
5 Government policy chief
9 "Time for me to go!"
14 Wrathful "Star Trek" villain
15 Karate shop?
16 Kathmandu's country
17 Tom Waits song about the past
20 Ocelot, for Dalí
21 Alternative to rouge, when making a roulette bet
22 "Later!"
23 About 2 o'clock, on a compass
24 Reddit Q&A session
25 Ramadan observer's faith
26 Not at all colorful
28 Bill worth 100 smackers
30 Hookups in the hosp.
33 Org. with slide rules?
35 Abbr. on an e-ticket
36 Sound at a salon
37 Kylie Minogue song about the present
42 Owned by all of us
43 Dinghy thingy
44 How-___ (instructional videos)
45 It might be under a tank
46 Emulate a peacock
48 Occipital ___ (part of the brain)
51 State whose lowest point is in Lewiston
53 Sex ed subj.
55 "But ___ Cheerleader" (1999 Natasha Lyonne film)
57 Piece together, as film
59 Part of Miss Muffet's menu
60 ___-Manuel Miranda ("Tick, Tick ... Boom!" director)
61 With 69-Across, Bob Dylan song about the future
64 Dior design of the 1950s
65 Trumpeter Al
66 Twisting Winter Olympics leap
67 Went a few rounds
68 Prepares to play the cello
69 See 61-Across

DOWN

1 Zoom alternative
2 Famous last words?
3 Popular time for an egg roll
4 Minecraft explosive
5 Floppy disk successor
6 Celestial coordinate system
7 Cracked just a little
8 Rogers who rode Trigger
9 Dr. Scholl's purchase
10 Three Tenors conductor Zubin
11 Receptive attitude
12 Card game that sounds like an Egyptian ruler
13 Took wing
18 Encourage, as someone's self-destructive behavior
19 Word before replay or message
25 Fourth Greek vowel
27 Quantities: Abbr.
29 India's first prime minister
31 By way of
32 Intelligence seeker
34 Luke, to Leia
36 Not bad
37 Barker succeeded by Carey
38 E.U. member?: Abbr.
39 Backpack snack
40 Pacific root crop
41 "See!"
46 Regarded with reverence
47 Charity fun run souvenir
49 "___ Blues" (Neil Simon play)
50 First rapper to win an Oscar for Best Original Song
52 Mother of Aphrodite
54 They're held for questioning
56 Protractor measurement
57 Shot-in-the-dark guess
58 Traveler Marco
59 "Band of Brothers" setting, briefly
62 Surprised sounds
63 Back muscle, for short

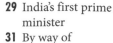

THE WORST THANKSGIVING EVER!

BY ADESINA O. KOIKI

ACROSS

1 Brazilian dance with African roots
6 Trudge
10 Petitions
14 Online missive
15 Toni Braxton once portrayed her on Broadway
16 Go dry, like lips
17 What we ate after dad took the entrée out of the oven early to watch the game?
19 Cheat on a test, say
20 Go downhill fast, in a way
21 Absorbed, as a cost
22 Anti-harassment movement
23 Situation after my aunt tripped over our dog while carrying a side dish?
27 One of 400,000 promised (but never delivered) to former black slaves in an 1865 order
29 Muscle Beach types
30 "Take a hike!"
31 Palindromic horn sound
33 "A Different World" actress Jasmine
36 What my brother shouted when I forgot to put crust on top of my dessert?
40 Jazz icon Montgomery
41 ___ vera
42 Financial wherewithal
43 Subtle hair dye jobs
46 Kunis of "Family Guy"
47 What my unapologetic uncle said after smothering everything on his plate with heaps of sweet potatoes?
52 Nickname for Ignacio
53 Tax-deferred retirement plan: Abbr.
54 Tax preparation expert: Abbr.
57 The last word of "O Canada"
58 What my nephew turned part of my wife's wedding dress into after a clumsy sauce accident?
62 Loud response
63 ___-Me (small clone)
64 How some people like their toast
65 First place, twice over
66 Muscat is its capital
67 Doesn't hide?

DOWN

1 Sixty in a min.
2 Uncontrollably and disruptively
3 African country with 13 national languages
4 "The Price Is Right" guess
5 Ctrl-___-Del
6 Divides with a comb or hair trimmer
7 Modern measures of popularity
8 Work with an honoree
9 Same-___ delivery
10 Yield by giving consent
11 Attempt to score
12 Comic-book sound effect
13 Watch stealthily
18 Dubai locale: Abbr.
22 "Grand" letters in Las Vegas
23 "Jiminy Christmas!"
24 Name on a cognac bottle
25 "Fingers crossed!"
26 ___ pot (sinus-cleaning device)
27 Feel intense desire
28 Crab or lobster
30 U-turn from NNE
31 "Black Wall Street" setting
32 Spanish "gold"
34 Forearm bone
35 U-turn from "no"
37 Solemn promise
38 Eponymous Jane Austen heroine
39 Common suffix in German and Norwegian city names
44 Shout upon an arrival
45 Popular pro wrestling stable in the late 1990s: Abbr.
47 IUD component?
48 Google rival
49 Disney's first Black princess
50 Michael ___, Hall of Fame wide receiver who caught six career touchdowns on Thanksgiving Day
51 Exclamation of joy or success
54 Show empathy
55 "Get the Party Started" singer
56 Insects on a hill
58 Engineered crop letters
59 What a shot that's "nothing but net" doesn't touch
60 Atlanta-based TV initials
61 Regret

VIBE CHECK

BY WILL NEDIGER

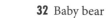

ACROSS

1 Jack who could eat no fat
6 Guard dog's warning
10 "So cute!"
13 Union member?
14 Team on a farm
15 Aegean, e.g.
16 *Dining experience with lots of small dishes*
18 When the credits roll
19 Embroidery or sculpture
20 *Don't wait for someone to reply to your message*
22 They might flare during an argument
24 Outfits
26 App customer
27 Sharpen
30 Mindful attention
31 Santa Claus
34 Board game with a turtle strategy
36 Coldest temperature of the day
37 *Something signed in the lobby*
40 Chuckling syllable
43 Wrestling commentator Phoenix
44 Relatives of aunts or uncles

48 Unreturned tennis serves
50 Sound of a failed attempt to skip a stone
52 Traveled on horseback
53 Complicated situation
55 Strong encouragements
58 *Substack publication*
61 Anti-trafficking org.
62 "Après ___, le déluge" ("After me, the flood")
63 Pick up on what people are thinking ... or a hint to the answers to this puzzle's italicized clues

65 Thurman of "The House That Jack Built"
66 "Supposing that's true ..."
67 Build up over time
68 Place to do some heavy lifting
69 Editor's "Leave it as is"
70 Talk a big game

DOWN

1 Most minimalist
2 Male carriers
3 Day-in-day-out routine
4 Comment that breaks the fourth wall
5 General tone of a conversation
6 Do terribly at the box office

7 "Beverly Hills Cop" protagonist
8 Fails to honor, as a promise
9 Notre Dame football coach Rockne
10 One who might wear a black ring on the middle finger
11 Started playing for money
12 Huge roll of cash
13 Standing in society
17 Effusively dole out compliments
21 "... yadda yadda yadda," briefly
23 Stuffy person
25 Make shifts, e.g.
28 Prefix meaning "straight"
29 Important part of a pen

32 Baby bear
33 Stays out of the right lane
35 Pond swimmer
38 Cards' city: Abbr.
39 BET Award winner Hilson
40 Over-the-top actor
41 "In this ___?"
42 Start of the chorus to "Rock You Like a Hurricane"
45 World's largest birds of prey
46 Just barely defeat
47 Type of seeds in gomashio
49 Tool that can be used as a musical instrument
51 Shot on the green
54 Certain antidepressants, for short
56 Title of songs by Rihanna and Amy Winehouse
57 ___-Roman wrestling
59 Simplicity
60 Nickname for Toronto
62 Cup that might have a family picture on it
64 Record label for Britney Spears

SOUNDS COOL!

by Andrew J. Ries

ACROSS

1 Chipmunk voiced by Andy Samberg in a 2022 movie
5 "In a way"
10 Fall (off)
14 On the sheltered side, in nautical terms
15 Often-polarizing figure for a sports team
16 Lynch who hosted "Hollywood Game Night"
17 Elephant's long tooth
18 Kraken, for one
20 Mtn Dew ___ (energy drink)
21 Molecule with a spare electron, say
22 Greek letter that resembles a trident
23 Channel with much reality programming
24 Paragon of slowness
26 "Let Me Down Slowly" singer ___ Benjamin
27 Music to a massage therapist's ears
28 Wisconsin city that translates to "clear water"
31 Kevin in the Theater Hall of Fame
33 Prefix with health or commute
34 Except
35 Partially obscured
36 Chilly stretch ... and the end result of the shaded squares?
39 Maritime menace
42 Balloon filler
43 McKinnon who was on "SNL" for 11 seasons
47 Far from proficient
48 Iconic cliff in Yosemite National Park
50 Prompt for an actor
51 Very top
53 Make changes to, as a law
54 Victor over HOU in the 2021 World Series
55 Spider's creation
56 Bond, for one
58 Comic Wong
59 Top-billed star of "The Howling," "Cujo," and "E.T."
62 Birthday-sharing sibling
63 Black-and-white beast
64 "The Merry Widow" composer Franz
65 Chill
66 Turns moldy, perhaps
67 Snide grin
68 Needle holes

DOWN

1 Statistician's compilation
2 Graduates from one of the Seven Sisters, e.g.
3 Musician with a Gibson line of guitars named for him
4 "Yikes!"
5 Just okay
6 Poet Wilfred
7 Messenger ___
8 House of worship
9 Came up
10 Nightclub spinners
11 Hairstyle named for a vermin appendage
12 Like some narrow roads
13 On a roost, perhaps
19 Coin with Monticello on the back
21 Under the weather
25 Very large glacier
26 Opportunity to buy oils and such
29 Competent
30 T-shaped birth control device: Abbr.
32 "No Time" rapper (1996)
35 Fashion designer Wang
37 Locale of the National Gallery of Canada
38 Insta upload
39 Lance-wielding bullfighter
40 Nirvana's follow-up to "Nevermind"
41 Verb on many political signs
44 Eroded
45 Sunning creation
46 The movie "Clue" includes three of them
48 Iconic image
49 Compensation
52 Spreadsheet array
56 Mark of an injury
57 Job benefit
60 "When I ___ your age ..."
61 Tuna often seared
62 Not merely "a"

'TIS THE SEASON

BY PATRICK BLINDAUER

ACROSS

1 Does some holiday spending, say
6 Card quartet member
9 Perform "A Visit from St. Nicholas," for example
14 "Peace on ___" (U2 song)
15 ___ Surprise! (line of dolls whose appeal I do not comprehend)
16 Speedcuber or competitive eater
17 1984 sci-fi film starring Robert Preston as video game designer Centauri
20 "Now the jingle hop ___ begun ..."
21 Sound made during the farm animal game Snorta!
22 Celebrity chef Garten
23 Sends a quick text
24 Certain floral arrangements
25 "Peter Pan" character whose performer often doubles as the Crocodile

27 "Tough luck!"
30 Reacted to a booster, perhaps
34 Tan shades
35 "Good Times" actress Rolle
36 "The reason for the season," some say
37 With 31-Down, holiday greeting
38 Letters before Pinafore
39 Anna of fashion
40 Sign in a store window
42 Sound preceding a secret
45 Wong of "Big Mouth"
46 Middle digit of most ZIP codes in Beverly Hills
47 Rogues, for example

52 "This is Calcutta. ___ is dead" ("Rent" lyric)
56 Little snitch
57 Cork can be found at the bottom of it
58 Goes off on
59 Makes connections
60 Starting soccer score
61 Driving aid: Abbr.

DOWN

1 MacFarlane who cites Rex Harrison as the inspiration for Stewie's voice on "Family Guy"
2 Gag reflex?
3 Resources on Catan cards
4 Tammy Faye's former org.

5 Like some plugs
6 What a choir requires
7 One sharing top billing
8 Like Legolas
9 Creatures, and a word you shouldn't leave the NI out of
10 Kin of sis, boom, or bah
11 Broadway opening?
12 Abound (with)
13 Messes up
18 Messes up
19 Mightily impressed
24 Chickpea, for one
26 Chip in, in a way
27 Follower of a prep.
28 "___ Haw" (classic TV variety show)

29 Messages for 40-Down
31 See 37-Across
32 Musket attachment?
33 Word before mouth or goods
40 Mommy kisser of song
41 Jennifer Garner show that garnered her four Emmy nominations
43 Porcine farm animals
44 Mr. ___ Wild Ride
48 Zealous fan, slangily
49 Et ___ (and others)
50 Carter of "Gimme a Break!"
51 Univ. applicants, typically
52 Keane of comic strips
53 Not a reproduction: Abbr.
54 Untidy pile
55 New Haven student body, slangily

SOLVING FOR X-MAS

BY ADESINA O. KOIKI

ACROSS

1 CEO's degree, often
4 Dropped
8 Jackie Chan's "Rush Hour" co-star
14 White clerical vestment
15 Like Girl Scout "Mints"
16 "Smallville" actress Huffman
17 Gulf of Mexico port city
19 Toddler's shoe fastener
20 Arbitrator's judgment
21 Org. in "Judas and the Black Messiah"
23 Mr. ___ (character during the second season of "Lost")
24 Far-reaching
25 Krispy ___ (doughnut chain)
27 OPEC measures: Abbr.
29 Basic skiing technique used for turning
31 Online abbr. for "not online"
33 Form attachment?
34 Poetic feet
36 Made from a cereal grain
38 Danish physicist who pioneered the study of electromagnetism
43 Rap battle combatant
44 Muscat native
45 Drone regulators: Abbr.
46 ___-mo replay
49 Full of subtlety
53 Word in a Gillette brand name
55 Ultimate villain
57 "Say Anything ..." actress Skye
58 "Me" problem, say
59 Speed Wagon company
60 Tiny flying insects
61 Wood surface applications
63 Best Actress of 1965 for "Darling"
66 A bank may waive one
67 Lionel train track shape
68 Make a mistake
69 Talks at great length
70 Sisterhood name in a 1996 novel/2002 film
71 Movie-making venue

DOWN

1 Long-tailed parrots
2 Waste an opportunity
3 Rub up against
4 Target for a drywall nail
5 Gap fillers, of sorts
6 Put the kibosh on
7 Potato peeler for those without an actual potato peeler
8 "X-Men" professor
9 Mod or nod ender?
10 "Pretty Little Liars" main character
11 Perform exceptionally
12 Course registrant
13 "The Serpent and the Rope" author Raja
18 Starting proposition
22 Weight-to-height ratio: Abbr.
25 ___ Räikkönen, 2007 Formula One world champion known as "the Iceman"
26 Country music icon who played Annie in a Broadway revival of "Annie Get Your Gun"
28 Playing surface for some volleyball matches
30 Horizontal reference lines
32 ___ Doone (square-shaped cookie)
35 ___-cone (flavored ice treat)
37 Beyond ridiculous
38 Weightiness
39 Sweet, almond-flavored liqueur
40 The Rose Bowl, e.g.
41 Luxury hotel chain
42 Waters: French
47 Don of 1956 World Series perfect-game fame
48 Any nonzero number raised to the power of zero
50 Persuades
51 Unabridged
52 Sandstorm location
54 Elaborate hairstyles
56 Beethoven's "Ode___"
60 River with a namesake "monster"
61 Old ottoman problem
62 "The Matrix Resurrections" role
64 Sch. in Charlottesville
65 Build a nest egg?

SWITCHING SIDES

BY WILL NEDIGER

ACROSS

1 Opt for
7 Without much moisture
10 Consoles bundled with a popular sports game
14 Mariam's partner in music
15 Sense of visual discrimination
16 Public Ivy that announced in 2022 it would leave the Pac-12
17 Giles Corey and John Proctor?
19 Mineral in baby powder
20 Terminal degrees in many fields
21 Sounds from ewes
22 Royal ___ (cookie brand whose tins are often used to store sewing supplies)
23 ___ Paulo
24 Diminutive
25 Dinged up
26 Knife that needs sharpening?
28 Negative response at boot camp
31 Enter a number, on a rotary phone
32 Spanish "Hey!"
33 Spanish "eight"
34 Bass-baritone role in a George Gershwin opera
36 Serenades and plies with flowers, e.g.
37 Prefix for pronouns
38 Creation at camp
39 Division between family and species
40 Rapper with poetic verses?
44 Buries
45 Animals in many "Far Side" strips
46 Show with musical guests, for short
49 "Chad" creator Pedrad
50 Suffix with kitchen or luncheon
51 Cleveland's state
52 Partner of sciences
53 "Dune" and others?

55 Rise up in the streets
56 MGM's roaring mascot
57 Ventures out in, as cold weather
58 Doesn't shut up
59 Pachinko parlor currency
60 Job negotiation topic

DOWN

1 Expressions in many YouTube thumbnails
2 Nebraska's biggest city
3 Well-hidden character in children's books
4 ___ of March
5 Holland with an iconic "Lip Sync Battle" appearance
6 Word from Scrooge
7 "Oh, *now* I get it," e.g.
8 Breads that might be marbled
9 "Indeed"
10 "Enter the ___ (36 Chambers)" (classic 1993 album)
11 Melodramatic cry of exhaustion
12 "Till next time"
13 Loose-fitting garment
18 "Avatar: The Last Airbender" protagonist
22 Hand out playing cards
24 Standard at a golf course
25 The Normandy landings, casually

26 ___ de Janeiro
27 Really like
28 Like Angel on "Craig of the Creek"
29 Display tanks with sharks
30 Position between second and third base
34 Things taken with a cam
35 Brutish Middle-earth resident
36 Spider's insect trap
38 Relatively hard, as tofu
39 Soldiers
41 Believers in a "watchmaker God"
42 Military prep program on campus
43 Nerds
46 Member of the Trimurti
47 More pleasant
48 Like some data compression
50 Sword with a large bell guard
51 Australia's national gemstone
53 Sneaky
54 You might usher in a new one

GET A LOAD OF THIS!

BY ANDREW J. RIES

ACROSS

1 Flying toy
5 Piano recital piece
11 WWII hero Hayes
14 Age after Stone and Bronze
15 Released to the public, as confidential info
16 Neither/___
17 Broad articles of formal menswear
19 French filmmaker Besson
20 Send out
21 There are 2.54 of them in an inch: Abbr.
22 Sworn statement
23 Emulate an adventure story protagonist, say
27 Stick on a car
30 "The Phantom of the ___"
31 Comic Bill
32 Extra payment
34 Low areas between mountains
37 College website address ending
38 "Uncultivated" grass that may be used in a whiskey grain bill
41 Got some nourishment
42 Pace
44 In addition
45 Vogue editor-in-chief Wintour
46 Charity golf tournament format, often
49 Plans divided into minutes
51 Framework installed in a construction zone
53 Not in
54 Paxlovid authorizer: Abbr.
55 Hottest planet in the solar system
59 "I don't know ___": Mariah Carey, in a much-shared clip
60 Lengthy compilation ... which is made up by this puzzle's shaded squares?
63 Strange
64 Vessel containing lubricant
65 Nickname for a midwestern capital city
66 Exclamation accompanying a fist pump
67 Dog show categories
68 Try to convince

DOWN

1 Fuzzy fruit
2 Colorful part of the eye
3 Heaps and heaps
4 Ultimate consumer
5 ___-pitch softball
6 Elided word in "The Star-Spangled Banner"
7 "Of course," in noir slang
8 Angled outward, as arms
9 Prepares to drive, in a way
10 Premium subscribers may be able to bypass them
11 Dreaming, say
12 Google Maps formulation
13 Highlight of the St. Louis skyline
18 Basted, say
22 Fried side dish at a barbecue joint
24 Opposition side
25 Flapper on a boat
26 Give up
27 Help with a job
28 In one's birthday suit
29 Important holdings for bridge players
33 Summertime clock setting on the West Coast: Abbr.
35 Site of multiple May 2023 eruptions
36 Salty waters
38 Sound from a dog kennel
39 ___ trip
40 Practitioner of meditation
43 Make an entreaty to a deity
45 Like cherubs
47 Act of cheating
48 Space station unit
50 You can go green with it
51 Prime Minister Ulf Kristersson, for one
52 *NSYNC alum Bass
53 Marina greeting
56 Boy, in Baja
57 Government department concerned with farming: Abbr.
58 River of the underworld, in Greek myth
60 Soft toss
61 Palindromic family member
62 ICU VIPs

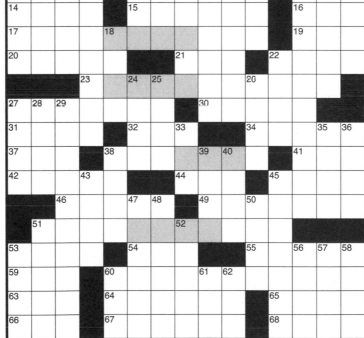

BLOOD DONOR

BY PATRICK BLINDAUER

ACROSS

1 Rock out
4 Ballpark figs.
8 Knee-to-ankle bone
14 "I'm ___ payphone trying to call home" (Maroon 5 lyric)
15 Chaplin of "Game of Thrones"
16 Lover of Aphrodite
17 "Help me with a crime?," put another way?
20 Modern missives
21 Part of a downsizing plan, say
22 Him, to Henri
23 Allows to enter
25 "Hooray!" relative
27 "He ___ Game" (Spike Lee joint)
30 Low digit that isn't ONE or TWO
31 "___ Everybody" (Drive Shaft song from "Lost")
34 Cousin of a weasel
36 Dove's dwelling
39 Hoops tourney org.
40 Security floodlights, for example?
43 ___: Chronicles of Empire & Exile (board game)
44 1952 Winter Olympics host
45 Pool events
46 Cannon ammo, at times
48 Quick time out?
50 "Gloria in excelsis ___" (Christmas carol chorus)
51 U.S. drug safety org.
52 Rice dish whose name means "frying pan"
55 Ewe in the movie "Babe"
57 Graceful seabird with a forked tail
59 City near Mt. Rainier
63 Power of one who leaves things out?
66 "___ Train" (1980 horror movie starring Jamie Lee Curtis)
67 One of two for George R.R. Martin: Abbr.
68 Fez, for one
69 "Have a sample!"
70 Draws to a close
71 Blood typing letters ... and what's been donated to 17-, 40-, and 63-Across

DOWN

1 Gemstone used by Chinese carvers
2 Bohr-ing unit of matter
3 Rudolph of "Big Mouth"
4 Ball game?
5 Greets by bending at the waist
6 ___ jiffy (quickly)
7 Christian singer Patty
8 Destiny
9 Phrase of agreement
10 Feathery neckwear for Miss Piggy
11 Like some linen
12 In ___ of (instead of)
13 Italian bubbly source
18 Crude stuff
19 Element with the symbol Sn
24 Factions of the faithful
26 Sudden forward thrust, in fencing
27 Sexual area named for Dr. Ernst Gräfenberg
28 Others, in Oaxaca
29 Fictional canine collector
31 Gen-___ (millennial)
32 Cappuccino cousin
33 Prop in "The Will Rogers Follies"
35 Insect also known as a greenfly
37 Olive ___
38 Steakhouse offering
41 Fall prey to decay
42 Surgical installations
47 Betrays, informally
49 "Curiously strong" mint
52 Not an amateur
53 Best Musical winner between "A Chorus Line" and "Ain't Misbehavin'"
54 Move forward on a decision
55 Abolitionist Lucretia
56 Pt. of ASL
58 Emerald Isle, in one of its languages
60 "Jaws" boat
61 Utah city near Arches
62 Greyhound fare?
64 Letters for a hit Broadway show
65 Cable channel founded in 1980

GETTING IN SHAPE

BY ADESINA O. KOIKI

ACROSS

1 ___ point (common dog marking)
4 Kids in the fam
8 Like some promises or threats
13 Assured of success
14 Sansa's sister on "Game of Thrones"
15 ___ Ko, youngest player to be ranked #1 in professional golf (17 years old)
16 American city, lake, or tribe
17 Return
19 Went kaput
20 24-hr. TV marketplace
21 Stockpile
22 Inept
25 Hair shade?
26 Card game declaration
27 Stat that's often 30 or 50
30 Insured patient's expense
33 In close confrontation
35 Like most graffiti, briefly
36 YouTubers' uploads
38 Skateboarding shoe manufacturer
39 Beat badly
41 Wards (off)
42 Code for New York's Hancock International Airport
43 2021 M. Night Shyamalan thriller
44 Mars domain?
45 Sordid affair, perhaps
51 Certain European ... or a European vegetable
53 ___ cannon ("Star Wars" weapon)
54 Smooth out the wrinkles
55 Where many UFC matches are staged
57 Fortify, as one's loins
58 Digestive aid brand
59 Sasquatch relative
60 Zero's opposite, in a way
61 Seller of TV plugs
62 5-Down Gaelic language
63 Score in rugby

DOWN

1 "Deja Vu (Uptown Baby)" hip-hop duo Lord ___ and Peter Gunz
2 Vowel-rich goodbye
3 "Can I help?"
4 Small perfumed bag
5 Word before setter or coffee
6 Talking Heads lead singer David
7 Pouch, biologically
8 He or I, but not him
9 "I'm sorry about that!"
10 BlackBerries, e.g.
11 Muscular twitches
12 Chatter away
13 Rx orders
18 They're first, in a phrase
23 Beam of light
24 Excited
27 Overzealous follower
28 Small fishing spot
29 Admit, with "up"
30 Truck sections
31 Just (the amount specified)
32 Rain cats and dogs
33 Enormous quantity
34 FedEx shipping option
36 Luxurious softness
37 Miner's jackpot
40 One with a sympathetic demeanor, in a negotiation tactic
41 Org. with many workers in control towers
44 ___ Harlow, first model with vitiligo to walk in the Victoria's Secret Fashion Show
45 Sierra ___
46 2022 Chinese zodiac animal
47 "Back to My ___" (1993 club hit by RuPaul)
48 Foxy Brown and Jackie Brown portrayer Pam ___
49 Londoner's truck
50 High-quality weed, in the cannabis world
51 Backyard workshop
52 TLC's "What Not to ___"
55 Not yet scheduled, briefly
56 What the pros say?

LOOK INSIDE

BY WILL NEDIGER

ACROSS

1 Political corruption
6 Say "I'm busy that day," e.g.
10 Makes a choice
14 Bit of Russian money
15 America's Cup trophy, e.g.
16 Ripped
17 Love, in Lyon
18 "The Power of the Dog" director Campion
19 Dino on the "Jurassic Park" poster
20 Country with a centralized government / Exaggerate
23 Lead-in to "fix"
24 Response to a shocking text
25 Fix a stuffed animal that's falling apart, say
26 Scare off / Immediately
32 Facility
35 Puts on TV again
36 Smallest positive integer
37 Fashion house with the Miu Miu brand
39 Numbered highway, for short
40 Reaction on Twitch

42 "Gross!"
43 Handles the helm
46 Work in Google Docs, maybe
47 Survived against all odds / Possible fate of the universe
50 Zilch
51 In need of water
52 Computer programmer Lovelace
55 Places for victorious jockeys / What to pay attention to in order to make sense of the second halves of the two-part clues
60 It might be written on a restaurant blackboard

61 ___ Wars (Pepsi/Coke rivalry)
62 Opera selections
63 Electronic musician who has worked with Björk and FKA twigs
64 "I get it already!"
65 Zora ___ Hurston
66 Ring out like a bell
67 Silence in a Zoom call
68 Trial runs

DOWN

1 Manage to understand
2 Something heard through the grapevine
3 Clichéd rhyme for "love" in poems

4 Chimney passageway
5 Intense fear
6 Fiddled with
7 Goodies in a goody bag
8 ___ diagram
9 News conference, casually
10 Where Justin Trudeau works
11 Left on a boat
12 Place for a backyard house
13 Rarity in children's movies
21 Qatari leader
22 Past, present, or future
26 Put money in, as a parking meter
27 Despised
28 Traditional wedding dessert
29 Something to knock on

30 ___disestablishmentarianism
31 Throw with great force
32 ___ bacon (epitome of early 2010s internet humor)
33 Triumphal monument
34 "For Pete's ___!"
38 Sean who played Sam Gamgee in "The Lord of the Rings"
41 "Not great, not terrible"
44 Biz with phones
45 Dress draped over the shoulder
48 Happening every year
49 Cruel ruler
52 Something a hacker might use
53 Handed out cards
54 Donkeys
55 Word before "here" and "queer" in a Pride slogan
56 Cuzco-based empire
57 Streaming device maker
58 Place for a coin
59 Language with a Plains dialect
60 "Here be dragons" document

PLAYING DOUBLES

BY ANDREW J. RIES

ACROSS

1 Celebrity ride
5 Buggy operators
10 Amazes
14 Country currently ruled by Sultan Haitham
15 Harris debater in 2020
16 In concert
17 Diplomatic achievement
18 Drug in "Fear and Loathing in Las Vegas"
19 Still competing
20 Two MLB players = Protective spirit
23 Scooter brand
24 Composer Keszler
25 Under covers, maybe
27 Hot temper
28 Dish Network competitor
31 Legislator's call of support
32 Whole bunch
34 Language related to Aramaic
36 Two NFL players = Grizzly, for one
40 Ascent

43 Who Nixon called "the most dangerous man in America"
44 Condition that may be treated with a cream
48 Hospital areas
50 Singer-songwriter DiFranco
51 "Don Juan" poet
52 ___ pal
53 Activity for belting one out at a pub
56 Chewed up
57 Tree trunk coating
59 Starring roles
61 Two NBA players = Nickname for Louis XIV
63 Two NHL players = Queens-based budget airline

65 Tallinn is its capital
66 Another name for a hazelnut
67 Credit card bill listings
68 Worked, as dough

DOWN

1 Cut (off)
2 Feast for the mind's eye
3 Apple picker?
4 Not served from a bottle, at a bar
5 Did an impression of
6 Area of expertise
7 Take a deep breath
8 Visually stunning
9 Mount Olympus queen
10 Orient

11 Business with red and white options
12 Look while throwing shade, say
13 Fully prepared
21 Weather forecaster's tool
22 Brand with "Essentially Enriched" products
23 Partner of vigor
26 Drops in the morning
29 Object of veneration
30 Pronoun with singular and plural forms
33 "Yeah, that's completely believable"
35 Noise from an ass
37 Depreciation from use

38 Grammy, alternately
39 High energy
40 Floor protector
41 With no time to spare
42 Feature of the words "bread" and "aisle"
45 Lovingly held
46 "I could be wrong"
47 Atlanta-to-Charlotte direction: Abbr.
49 Mikaela Shiffrin's sport
51 Boll weevil, for one
54 Murphy of "Schitt's Creek"
55 Journalist Ezra
58 Toffee-and-chocolate confection
60 Group that inspired "Mamma Mia!"
61 Brief moment of time, informally
62 Lawnmower fuel
63 Prez during the "Camelot era"
64 Boarding pass info: Abbr.

ABOUT FACE

BY PATRICK BLINDAUER

ACROSS

1 "When You Wish Upon ___"
6 Page in an atlas
9 Chaplin's were baggy
14 Opening chapter
15 Lovelace of early computing
16 Constellation also known as the Hunter
17 Lead weight
18 Something to do in a certain suit
19 Ford model named for a horse
20 Lancelot du ___ (knight of the Round Table)
21 Retribution policy
24 Civil War general Stuart
25 Utopian place
27 Sporting event venue
28 Rocks out
29 Choose to participate, with "in"
31 Part of some flapper costumes
33 Third planet from the sun
36 Prefix with Cat or cone

39 Cheerless, to poets
43 Bow's husband on "Black-ish"
44 Got clean, say
47 Itinerary preposition
48 "___ idiot!" ("Silly me!")
50 Very cushy class
51 Ice mass, for short
52 "Behold!"
53 Give a majority of the vote
54 Concerning, on a memo
55 Turned blue, maybe
57 "Good Luck to You, ___ Grande"
58 "Hold ___ your hats!"
59 Tiny unit of data
60 Yoga class syllables

62 Stanley Cup awarder
64 Monotonous routine
66 1990 Kline/Ullman dark comedy
70 Korbut of gymnastics
71 Haul to the police station
72 Seed of innovation
73 "Any minute now"
74 Make amends (for)
75 Hatching post

DOWN

1 Russet or winesap
2 Leaves on the side?
3 Suspension of hostilities

4 Cashpoint, in the U.S.
5 Prime steak cut
6 College declaration
7 Be crazy for
8 Like many ancient rituals
9 Spinach-gobbling sailor
10 Radio host Shapiro
11 Ancient Japanese mercenary
12 Spiritual emblem of a clan
13 Self-important sorts
22 Liposuction target
23 Suddenly seize
26 Part of NSFW
28 Nutella holder
30 Prof's degree, often

32 Unmatched, as socks
33 Do film cutting
34 Mammal that rolls into a ball
35 All set
36 Dies, as an engine
37 "Long time ___!"
38 Cousin of Percocet
40 Equitable transaction
41 Designated paths for aviators
42 Seething state
45 Extra-wide shoe spec
46 Put away, in a way
49 Highlands denial
51 Composting receptacle
56 Female koala
58 Word before hat or hand
59 Short personal histories
61 Gore Vidal novel "___ Breckinridge"
63 Refine, as a skill
65 Pointer's word
67 Undercover surveillance vehicle, perhaps
68 One, in Spain
69 A, in Germany

CAN I HAVE YOUR DIGITS?

BY ADESINA O. KOIKI

ACROSS

1 Go through carefully
5 Previously, in some dialects
10 Org. created to secure the U.S. bid to host the 1994 FIFA World Cup
13 Cuba, por ejemplo
14 Bowling alley features
15 Swamp buildup
16 Portable storage device
18 New Age music megastar
19 Dispatch boat of yesteryear
20 Packed in?
21 Considered, as a case
24 Speaker's aide, on many occasions
27 In a vulnerable position
29 Gets a 4.0, say
30 Cause irreparable damage to
31 The Brat Pack's Estevez
34 Weight gain associated with menopause
40 Ventilating shaft in a mine
41 Whirlpool
42 Grammy Award–winning Dutch DJ
45 Document endorser
47 Frequent sources of lecture interruptions
50 Influencer's concern
51 Item in a diary, for example
52 Trig function, essentially
54 Cause of brain freeze, sometimes
55 Promise
60 German philosopher Immanuel
61 1979 sci-fi film classic
62 Honeymoon, for one
63 The Hoosier State: Abbr.
64 Singer/actress Della
65 Mia who starred at UNC and on the U.S. Women's National Soccer Team

DOWN

1 Command at obedience school
2 Kinda
3 Annual shot target
4 Tangy tropical flavoring
5 German-owned supermarket chain
6 Persian language
7 Food item found in Philly cheesesteaks
8 Slam on the accelerator
9 Language suffix
10 "Baseball is 90 percent ___. The other half is physical": Yogi Berra
11 A story could have many of these
12 Tolerate
15 "I'm outie!"
17 Boxers not seen at the dog park, for short
20 Producer Gene Roddenberry or actor Dennis Farina, after their successful career changes
21 "No ___, no foul"
22 Decorative needle case
23 Parched
25 Strikes from the manuscript
26 Lives and breathes
28 Follow, as a schedule
32 Georgia birthplace of Little Richard
33 ___ Świątek, Three-time French Open women's champion
35 Full of vigor
36 Rogaine user's hoped-for outcome
37 Renowned chef Lewis who specialized in Southern cooking
38 Yemeni port city near the Red Sea
39 Colored artificially
42 Diced tomatoes packaging
43 Plan to do
44 Long-plumed heron
46 Bird mummified by ancient Egyptians
47 Japanese "energy healing"
48 Bert's "Sesame Street" bestie
49 "___ alive!"
53 Actress Daly of "The Enforcer"
55 Bogey beater
56 Infant addition?
57 Period of history
58 Accurate toothpaste label?
59 Wheel's speed: Abbr.

DISAMBIGUATION

BY WILL NEDIGER

ACROSS

1 Place to order a flat white
5 Finish shooting a film
9 Economic center of Iraq
14 Unpleasant
15 ___ Doktor Professor
16 Likely roster for an important match
17 This clue is about the Krzysztof Kieślowski film, not the color
19 Spanish Valentine's Day phrase
20 Airplane seat choice
21 Wise
23 "I couldn't agree more!"
24 Utterly ineffectual
26 This clue is about the Kendrick Lamar track, not the emotion
28 Center of attention
30 Bedard who voiced Pocahontas
31 Recipe amts.
34 Symbols of fertility in many traditions
37 Cold War spy agency
39 Letters before a nickname
40 This clue is about the Elie Wiesel novel, not the portion of a week
41 Latin for "I"
42 Fraction of a byte
43 FBI anti-corruption sting operation
44 PC game with a VR remake released in 2020
45 Lying belly-down
47 Cheese in spanakopita
49 This clue is about the two-player activity, not the bodily fluid
52 Agave product
56 Physicist Ernst with an eponymous number
57 Sita's husband
59 Cologne's river
60 Relatives of Tonys
62 This clue is about the dog breed, not the scientific research facility
64 "___ and the Sun" (Kazuo Ishiguro novel)
65 Requiring overtime, maybe
66 "Go Limp" singer Simone
67 ___-weensy
68 Non-main social media accounts
69 Trying hard to shock

DOWN

1 Like the song "Guantanamera"
2 ___ e olio (spaghetti dish with garlic and oil)
3 Hand that's all the same suit
4 Like the blind cave fish
5 "___ am I kidding?"
6 Guns the engine
7 Typeface that sounds like a car antenna
8 Italian "You're welcome!"
9 Echolocation user
10 Relaxed
11 Brine shrimp kept as a novelty pet
12 Soft-boiled items used as noodle toppings
13 Surrounded by
18 Cheesy sandwich
22 Sign of trouble
25 Patriarch in the Goldilocks story
27 "Three Pieces in the Shape of a Pear" composer Satie
29 Popular Welsh name
31 Something open in a browser
32 Like a relatively weak track on an album
33 Ancient Roman aristocrat
35 Easy as ___
36 Baker's production
38 It might be thwarted by a captcha
40 "Crud"
44 Device
46 Those not already listed
48 Bird that sounds like what you do with a car's steering wheel
49 Fire proof?
50 Island country with megalithic temples
51 "I hope this ___ finds you well"
53 Hardly courageous
54 Title character of a 1988 They Might Be Giants song
55 Pass on
58 Drive the getaway car for, maybe
61 For example
63 Pop-ups or banners

INSURANCE CARRIERS

BY ANDREW J. RIES

ACROSS

1 Screens at an airport
4 Appropriate
9 "The Company": Abbr.
12 Enlist for another tour of duty
14 Prince involved in "Megxit"
15 Provide capital to
16 Regulator of tee and club specifications: Abbr.
17 "Everything will be all right"
18 Varieties
19 Breakfast fare whose ingredients include eggs and potatoes
22 "Being and Nothingness" philosopher
23 Durance of "Smallville"
26 Hindu celebratory event in the springtime
31 Mecca for skiers
34 First part of a magician's rhyming phrase
35 "Pressure" singer Lennox
36 Use a spoon, in a way
37 Dot-over-dot symbol
38 Site of Vulcan's forge, per myth
39 "People ___ talking!"
40 Netflix crime series starring Omar Sy
41 Fencing tools
42 First label for the Rolling Stones
45 Act of imitation
46 Person who's tough to figure out
50 Alan Tudyk show about a spaceman who crash-lands on Earth
55 Puzzle solver's device, perhaps
57 Reporters and photographers and such
58 California city and valley
59 High-fat, low-carb diet
60 Port-au-Prince is its capital
61 Forget-me-___ (blue flowers)
62 Bleating mother
63 In many cases
64 Hurricane's center

DOWN

1 Set of beams that support a bridge
2 Vehicle brand that translates to "wasp"
3 Sweet grains
4 Tool that may be used with a mallet
5 Swearing-in statement
6 Words after an approximation
7 Event for seniors
8 Rug rat
9 Prepare for planting, as farmland
10 Printer insert
11 Streaming interruptions
13 Leopard or lion cousin
15 Guy who calls his aioli "donkey sauce"
20 Nutrient abundant in spinach
21 "We should do that!"
24 With 31-Down, grilled steak dish
25 Alternate handle
27 "That's my goal"
28 Type of acid in the vitamin B complex
29 ___ Lodge (budget hotel chain)
30 Connecticut's WNBA team
31 See 24-Down
32 Ailment affecting tonsils, for short
33 Freelancer's alternative to an hourly wage
37 Mean dog
38 Sororit-"E"?
40 Puts down, as a bet
41 "Hairspray" mother
43 Motto
44 Hold onto
47 Cobra-opposing fighter
48 Like an Italian sub
49 Flavoring in the Mexican liqueur xtabentún
51 Acronym with a humble/honest debate
52 Like many "CODA" characters
53 Clean language?
54 Nick at ___
55 Blues guitarist Zimmerman
56 Wedding attendee's assignment

THE NAME GAME

BY PATRICK BLINDAUER

ACROSS

1 Swear, informally
5 Dict. fill
8 Suddenly became attentive
13 English horn relative
14 ___-fly pie
15 Wipe clean
16 Animated girl with a map named Map
19 "I hate to ___ and run"
20 Hand-operated propeller
21 Cabinetry material
22 Musial of baseball fame
26 Member of a bar assoc.
30 One of four in Mississippi
31 Dylan's "It ___ Me, Babe"
33 Mother in wool
34 Hope of soccer fame
37 Range over 4,000 miles long
38 "Give ___ break!"
39 "Coloring Book" Grammy winner

43 Responds to on WhatsApp, say
44 How bedtime stories are read
45 Business env. marking
46 They come before sols
47 Singer/songwriter Aimee
48 W-2 info: Abbr.
50 Part of, as a scam
52 Illustrated feline created by American artist James Dean in 2008
57 Bouncer's requests, briefly
59 Issa who wrote "The Misadventures of Awkward Black Girl"
60 French for "summer"

61 Nautical role played by Robin Williams in a 1980 film
67 Power
68 Cry of pain
69 Charitable contributions
70 They might be bookmarked
71 Came face to face
72 Pinocchio's lie detector

DOWN

1 They may be cracked
2 "The Enemy Below" vessel
3 "... ish"
4 Place for SpongeBob's pineapple
5 One of journalism's five W's

6 Female fawn, e.g.
7 Follower of Red or White
8 Wall Street order
9 Pizzeria attraction
10 Road goo
11 Put into play
12 Unit-pricing word
14 Pre-Ayatollah rulers
17 Little tykes
18 One who writes
23 Element 10
24 Search for an escapee
25 Came through for
27 What some sirens do
28 Message with a hashtag, often
29 Hunger (for)
32 Org. checking carry-ons
34 Bradbury's genre
35 "You've got to be kidding!"

36 Rodeo rope
37 Show repentance
40 Filming device, for short
41 Pass, as time
42 Sheet in a door
48 Private supply
49 Where Willie Mays played his last season
51 Dorothy Gale, to Henry and Em
53 In an upright position
54 "Eleanor Rigby" instrument
55 Parts of molecules
56 Briefly worded
58 Some Easter supplies
61 Nightwear, for short
62 Yes, in Quebec
63 Car maintenance area
64 The piper's son of rhyme
65 Cherry or chartreuse
66 McShane of "American Gods"

78

LET THE UPSETS BEGIN

BY ADESINA O. KOIKI

ACROSS

1 ___-compliant (accessible for people with disabilities)
4 Confess
9 Researched item
13 Fearless
15 Pitt's role in 2011's "Moneyball"
16 Have muscle pains
17 Make an enemy of
19 Very brightly colored
20 What those unaffected by difficulties are said to lead
22 "M*A*S*H" location
23 Exceeded 65, perhaps
24 "I thought ___ never leave!"
27 MTV program originally hosted by Carson Daly, for short
30 Extinguish
32 Physician's "Now!"
36 Person who second-guesses other's decisions, informally
40 "You should join us!"
41 Amazing or saving follower
42 Boorish man
43 Discontinued Dodge SUV
45 Famed Mexican-American botanist Mexia
46 Boise State University home
47 Sub's boss
49 Windows web portal
50 Endure
54 World Golf Hall of Famer Lorena
59 NCAA Tournament colloquialism ... that also describes the starts of 20-, 36-, and 43-Across?
62 Betty's "Golden Girls" role
65 Nosebleed features?
66 Like Skeletor or the Decepticons (Where my '80s cartoon heads at?)
67 Turn up the melodrama
68 Genealogy diagram
69 Quick breath
70 Measured amounts
71 On the ___ (exactly on time)

DOWN

1 How someone may be taken
2 "Tiny Bubbles" crooner
3 Holy platform
4 Woodwind instrument
5 Meander
6 Pressed-on beauty accessories
7 Start to take off, in a way
8 Irritate
9 Air conditioner alternatives
10 High or low playing card
11 Comedian Margaret
12 Number of rings associated with Marvel superhero Shang-Chi
14 Truth or ___
18 Future MBA's hurdle
21 Ancient Icelandic literature
24 The "II" in HOMES
25 Suffix akin to "ish"
26 You owe them
28 Many a Ravi Shankar recording
29 Vowelless "Futurama" alien who rules the planet Omicron Persei 8
31 Greasy, in texture or in behavior
32 Theater backdrop
33 "Horned" amphibians
34 Middle East capital city
35 Silicon Valley's specialty, informally
37 GQ or SI, e.g.
38 Looped in, via email
39 Villain's foil
44 Spanish greeting
48 Chat room monitors, briefly
51 Moved with a curving trajectory
52 Joe ___
53 Greek god?
55 Website with gadget reviews
56 Learned through the grapevine
57 Relating to the bones: Prefix
58 Liability's counterpart
59 Succumb to the heat, say
60 Ending in chess
61 Mimics
62 Exercise unit
63 Fertility clinic collections
64 Unholy act

79

CRITICAL THINKING

BY WILL NEDIGER

ACROSS

1 Punctuation mark used in this clue, appropriately
6 House at the center of an estate
11 Short form that omits "etition" or "utation"
14 Do slightly better than
15 Remove from the chalkboard
16 Word in the Three Musketeers' motto
17 Paradoxically boring verve?
19 It might include your pronouns
20 Think highly of
21 Lad with courage?
23 Playfully mock
25 Radiates
26 Serving of food
30 Snake born from Medusa's blood
31 Pay for the table
32 Queeg : Caine :: ___ : Pequod
35 "Arcane" voice actor Purnell
39 "Critics have spoken" ... or a hint to what's been added to this puzzle's theme answers
42 Cat, casually
43 Byzantine princess and historian Comnena
44 Thesaurus creator
45 Minor complaint
47 Strict disciplinarians
49 Government, for short
52 "Truly, ___, Deeply" (1990 Alan Rickman movie)
54 "Ugh, I hate having to wear trousers"?
56 Compel
61 Call maker at a baseball stadium
62 "Next up, Edgar Allan Poe's masterpiece"?
64 Last letter of the alphabet, in the U.S.
65 Lauded Lauder
66 Chess champion Viswanathan
67 Last letter of the alphabet, in Canada
68 Prepare beans, in a way
69 Their stakes are low

DOWN

1 Use Python, e.g.
2 Big burden
3 Be emotionally touched
4 Hybrid animal similar to a hinny
5 Food drive?
6 "Women Without ___" (Shirin Neshat film)
7 Most Jordanians
8 Mother of pearl
9 Org. that mandates workplace testing
10 "The Matrix Resurrections" star
11 Expert on the Talmud
12 Author discussed in "My Life in Middlemarch"
13 Devious schemes
18 Parishioner's response
22 Type of butterfly or penguin
24 One more time
26 Letters in an address bar
27 Instrument in the huqin family
28 Some jeans
29 Root that's often roasted
30 Six-pack muscles
33 Barnyard layer
34 Fields Medal, for example
36 Material for a 114-foot-tall tower built in Milan
37 Committed perjury
38 Insects not found in Antarctica, ironically
40 Container bigger than a keg
41 Kid immersed in military culture
46 Less sensible
48 ___ vera
49 Filled with activity
50 "Turning Red" director Shi
51 Was visibly upset
52 Weekday headings on a calendar
53 Flower beloved by butterflies
55 Tapir's proboscis, e.g.
57 "Stay in your ___"
58 ___ the Terrible
59 Courteous guy
60 Wraps up
63 "Stop that!"

RETRO SHADES

BY ANDREW J. RIES

ACROSS

1 Wading bird with a curved bill
5 Swindles
10 Organization that advocates against age discrimination
14 Sample software version
15 Stand for a painter
16 "You're not telling the truth!"
17 Horse rider's woe
19 Force fighting a land war
20 Came to the surface
21 Division that includes the Las Vegas Raiders: Abbr.
23 Itch
24 Rob Manfred is its commissioner: Abbr.
26 Filmmaker Kurosawa
29 Shape whose internal angles each measure 135 degrees
34 Globe
35 "The Killing" star Mireille ___
36 High on the Scoville scale
37 Trade fair
40 ___ Allen (furniture chain)

42 Dispensers of 20s
43 Golf ball–holding peg
44 Staffer at a law firm, for short
45 Stereotypical name for a Lone Star State resident
47 "A Clockwork Orange" novelist
52 Part of a barcode reader
53 Old sock, perhaps
54 Energy
56 Enjoy an afternoon cup
60 Catherine with an Emmy for her role on "Schitt's Creek"
62 It's tracked by a bloodhound
64 2022 Pixar film ... and an explanation of the shaded squares?

66 Military installation
67 Mythological creature with 100 eyes
68 Care for
69 "___ Both Die at the End" (2017 YA novel)
70 Teensy bit
71 2/14, informally

DOWN

1 "In my opinion ..."
2 Be the ___ of bad news
3 "All finished!"
4 Installs turf on
5 Lay eyes on
6 Melon variety
7 Starting on
8 Nickname for Chicago's exchange, with "the"

9 Big number
10 "The Last Frontier"
11 Like an impenetrable seal
12 Player in 2022's Super Bowl
13 Ask personal questions, perhaps
18 Nocturnal creature of Madagascar
22 Grub
25 Its flagship Maine store features a giant boot sculpture
27 Space to maneuver
28 Insects that march
30 Sappy stuff
31 Post-surgery process

32 Lipstick ___ pig
33 In opposition to
37 Notation meaning "and others"
38 Warrior princess played by Lucy Lawless
39 Place where litter is bought and sold
41 Get a taste of
42 Firefighter's tool
44 Target of ire for a critic of government spending
46 Urge
48 Full-bodied
49 Planet with a laughed-at pronunciation
50 Let off the hook
51 Demi Singleton's role in "King Richard"
55 Rice-growing locale
57 Airport terminal calculations: Abbr.
58 Istanbul native
59 Therefore
61 "House Hunters" channel
62 Frequently
63 Headslap exclamation
65 Suffix in many nationalities

MUSICAL TRIO

BY PATRICK BLINDAUER

ACROSS

1 In the ___ of (among)
6 Handy piece of advice
9 Come together as a team
14 From Galway, say
15 "What ___, chopped liver?"
16 Like some annoying voices
17 Clandestine greeting upon meeting
20 Apropos
21 Carpenter's power tool
22 Traffic cops?: Abbr.
23 Like Oscar-winning actor Troy Kotsur
25 Verse's beginning?
26 Primate with a muzzle
28 Piece of information
30 TGIF segment
32 X-rated flick
33 Mono's successor
35 Hamilton's bill
37 At no time, in verse
38 Recite quickly from memory
41 Spitting sound
44 Knotted neckwear
45 Gave up, as one's rights
49 Deceptive ploys
51 Valvoline alternative
53 Big news on the sports page
54 Short form, for short
56 Refuel, in a way
58 Early Oscar winner Jannings
59 "Indeed!"
60 "Stranger Things" actress Dyer
63 Sash for a kimono
64 Instructions for one whose pants are on fire
67 Place for a corset
68 Small child
69 On the ocean blue
70 Agree to receive marketing emails
71 Season opposite hiver
72 "Gimme a break!"

DOWN

1 Gets the total wrong
2 Words of emphasis
3 Compose a letter, in a way
4 Ukr., Est. or Lith., once
5 Every now and ___
6 Falafel sandwich sauce
7 Kids' song with gestures
8 Notification sound
9 Open, like some jackets
10 "Ain't gonna happen!"
11 Animator Friz Freleng's birth name
12 Sign above some free samples
13 First Lady before Bess
18 Greek consonant
19 Honor with a knighthood, say
24 Storer of stoles
27 Big outdoor blaze
29 "Cry ___ River"
31 "Told you so!"
34 Baseball Hall of Famer Mel
36 Right this moment
39 "Deck the Halls" contraction
40 The 2% in 2% milk
41 Worships, say
42 Shoulderless shirt
43 PC connection point
46 Skedaddle
47 Some dispensary buys
48 Samson's betrayer
50 Forward, as mail
52 Roof of the mouth
55 Alternate spelling of a wd.
57 ___ Pan Alley
61 Big shopping bag
62 Call it ___ (retire)
65 Inflation abbr.
66 Rd. with a number

TAX SEASON

BY ADESINA O. KOIKI

ACROSS

1 Exam given face-to-face
5 Egyptian cobras
9 Not-as-expensive haircut option
13 Branch of math that includes De Morgan's laws
15 Breakfast chain with a blue roof
16 Operatic Ethiopian princess
17 Designed to fulfill two functions
19 "Truth be ___ ..."
20 Traveler's approximation: Abbr.
21 "Romeo Is Bleeding" actress Lena
22 Checked out thoroughly
24 Longtime cosmetics brand
25 Canadian gas pump brand
26 Having a bad effect on something
31 Martina's legendary tennis rival
32 Back of the neck
33 Informal assent
35 Leave in shambles
36 Southpaw
38 Ho Chi ___ City
39 Actress Thurman
40 Father, as a horse
41 Africa's second-longest river

42 Often-discussed basketball rule interpretation made into a popular meme involving non-sports videos
46 Sweethearts, informally
47 Traditional tales
48 Watering hole
51 Swing seat, maybe
52 Word before complex or mode
55 Site that began as AuctionWeb
56 "Schitt's Creek" co-creator
59 If's partner, in coding
60 What some "journalists" put on their news stories

61 ___ Montgomery, former WNBA player who is now vice president and part-owner of the Atlanta Dream
62 The lowest to win March Madness was #8 (Villanova, in 1985)
63 Run through a sieve
64 Have an inclination

DOWN

1 Antiquated "antiquated"
2 Cheer (for)
3 Rio Grande contents
4 Gay ___ (rights movement)
5 It abuts abetting

6 Deliberately ignore
7 Grass
8 Mad magazine comic strip
9 Henna is often used to make one
10 Major fracas
11 Like frivolous chatter
12 "No More Victims" org. advocating road safety
14 Prehistoric culture of North and Central America
18 North Carolina school whose mascot was the Fighting Christians, until 2000
23 90° from sur
24 Similar (to)

25 Coup d'___
26 Facebook's "like" button icon
27 Default font on Google Docs
28 Deduce from evidence
29 Prone to spinning yarns, say
30 Fencing maneuver
31 French vineyard designation
34 Soup that's the centerpiece of many eating contests
36 The "L" in NIL
37 Cupid's Greek equivalent
38 "Kiss Me ___" (Grammy-winning Doja Cat/SZA song)
40 "Lion King" baddie
41 Professional life
43 Took heed
44 Counsel recipient
45 Vuvuzela, for example
48 Concert merch
49 Willing companion?
50 Pottery piece for a bouquet
51 "Bring on the weekend!"
52 Unit of inheritance
53 Womb, in a metaphor
54 Became a blonde, say
57 News service org. founded in 1907
58 Tennis do-over

WHOA THERE!

BY WILL NEDIGER

ACROSS

1 Nickname for the Montreal Canadiens
5 Space on a schedule
9 Fasteners for doors
14 Meeker who promoted the Oregon Trail
15 "Buh-bye!"
16 Admit your mistakes
17 Party with chicken long rice
18 Furry "Star Wars" creature
19 List of candidates
20 Summertime rash
23 "Friend or ___?"
24 "In Search of Zora ___ Hurston" (Alice Walker essay)
25 Relationship for getting over your last relationship
27 Degree for Miuccia Prada
29 Sticky substance
30 Like some vaccines
31 Wi-Fi device
33 Grubhub alternative
37 2021 U.S. Open champion Raducanu
38 Crossword construction, to some

39 Catch a glimpse of
40 Spirit-boosting event at school
43 Shouted sharply
45 Shape of some sports fields
46 Homophone of "tin," if you have the pin-pen merger
47 Baseball team's best pitcher
48 Mariah Carey hit that samples "Genius of Love"
51 "A Little Devil in America" author Abdurraqib
53 Number that never goes down
54 "Slow down," or a description of 20-, 33-, or 40-Across
58 Cactus used in tacos

60 Lines on dresses
61 Shakespeare's river
62 Score on a test
63 One of the twelve in Twelver Shi'ism
64 "I ___ you so!"
65 Leaves on the table
66 Series about New York ball culture
67 Segments of history

DOWN

1 "I need assistance!"
2 Côte d'___ (French Riviera, in French)
3 Mind-decluttering technique
4 Sambal or sriracha

5 Absolutely fantastic
6 Brief worker
7 "Contrariwise," in a text
8 Become entrenched
9 Perk for a wedding guest
10 Pointy tool
11 Major muddle
12 Test out in a changing room
13 Movie that Homer Simpson thought was called "The Bus That Couldn't Slow Down"
21 Gender theorist Bornstein
22 Bubble-filled Nestlé product
26 More advanced in years

27 Do some kitchen work
28 Where the heart is, they say
32 Deck used for divination
33 Low in sugar
34 Say "Can you do something for me?"
35 Contractor's figure
36 Jekyll's alter ego
38 Efforts of privileged people to support less privileged people
41 Was of service
42 Caboose's place
43 "I have no idea!"
44 Actress Karina or literary character Karenina
46 Crapper who didn't actually invent the toilet
48 Dangerous canines
49 Ancient Greek public space
50 Birthplace of the Buddha
52 Ready to hit the roof
55 Jules Verne's undersea captain
56 RC trailer?
57 Farthest extremities
59 Palindromic 1990 civil rights law

BUSINESS FORMATION

BY ANDREW J. RIES

ACROSS

1 "Our boat is sinking!"
4 Structure that overhangs water
8 Letter-shaped house style
14 Snake in a "Cleopatra" scene
15 Highest point
16 Hardly gave it one's all
17 Semi-censored "Huh?!"
19 Event reported to the power company
20 Comic Silverman
21 Strict quality
23 Sought to win an election
24 Wireless phone service launched in 2015
26 Steeped beverage
29 Let out, as a secret
30 Bob Marley, for one
35 Ingredients in many cereals
37 Learn the ___ and outs
38 Member of the LDS Church
39 With 41-Across, gradually apparent problem ... and an explanation of the puzzle's shaded squares?
41 See 39-Across
42 Attractive appeal
43 Yoga class seating
44 Can't stand
45 2014 Best Picture nominee depicting a famous march
46 Flourish on a letter
48 Tyrannosaurus chaser?
49 Evergreen tree that can exceed 200 feet tall
52 Prefix that's half of "hex-"
55 Game with a drawing
56 "Robinson Crusoe" novelist Daniel
60 Comedy in which Jim Carrey stops saying no
62 Stick to one's guns
64 Nancy whose father was mayor of Baltimore
65 Law school newbie
66 Emeril interjection
67 Home to Ukraine's Potemkin Stairs
68 Connecticut town that's a homophone of a fruit
69 Like a fox, per a saying

DOWN

1 They have teeth but no mouth
2 Org. that makes inspections
3 Work on some punches
4 Pity-evoking feeling
5 I, in German
6 On the rise
7 They're free at fast food restaurants, typically
8 Emotionally icy
9 Long-range golf club that's not a wood
10 Snitch
11 Way off
12 Super big
13 Minneapolis suburb ___ Prairie
18 Instagram picture identifier
22 Form of toothpaste
25 Offer a view
26 Collegians may use sheets to make them
27 Country music great Steve
28 Coral ring that surrounds a lagoon
31 St. Louis icon
32 Ploy of dirty politics
33 Rich cake
34 Extension on a building
36 Done laps in a pool
38 Repeated artistic element
40 National Radio Hall of Fame inductee of 2014
41 Laughably unrealistic, as drawings
43 Aftershave additive
46 Took a load off
47 Bluegrass instrument
50 Ancient Greek region on the Aegean Sea
51 Traveling caller, perhaps
52 This cule features one
53 Netflix co-founder Hastings
54 Dot of land in a lake
57 Little lies
58 Taken through the mouth
59 Aspiration for a TV star
61 Mar. and Apr., e.g.
63 One of six spacecraft that made moon landings: Abbr.

RITZ HAMM ITSME
ERIE AREA NAMES
DEFROSTED TROMP
INFOR IKE EGGON
DES ZAC DARE
COOLMOUNTAIN
STAR LEI SEDUCE
NIVEA INC TATER
ONEACT EAR TOTO
WARMHANDLUKE
SIRI CSI HOE
TOTAL GNU LIENS
UHAUL HOTBODIES
SINCE TUTU EDIE
HOSES SNAG AILS

6 CLIMATE CHANGE AT THE MOVIES

7 YOU'RE STARTING TO SCARE ME!

ACT STIRUP MOET
GRO AIDING ONTO
EEO WOLFMANJACK
GOTWISETO BOP
ALIEN WTC PAR
PEEL REYNA MENU
LEELA CLEANS
GHOSTFACEKILLAH
MOREAU HELLA
OMIT TITLE NOSE
SEE HEN CIDER
NAG CISGENDER
WITCHDOCTOR MOO
EVER AMELIE AFL
DADE HERONS NFL

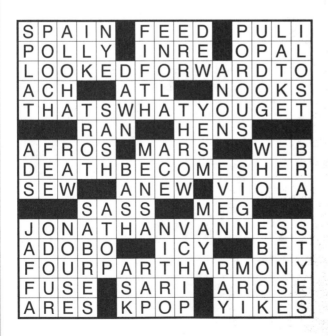

SPAIN FEED PULI
POLLY INRE OPAL
LOOKEDFORWARDTO
ACH ATL NOOKS
THATSWHATYOUGET
RAN HENS
AFROS MARS WEB
DEATHBECOMESHER
SEW ANEW VIOLA
SASS MEG
JONATHANVANNESS
ADOBO ICY BET
FOURPARTHARMONY
FUSE SARI AROSE
ARES KPOP YIKES

8 SYNCED UP

9 CAN I GET A WORD IN?

10 LUPITA SAYS

11 TOUCHDOWN DANCE

12 IT'S ALL RELATIVE

V	A	T	S		H	A	D		I	B	E	R	I	A
I	M	O	N		O	Z	U		C	E	D	A	R	S
S	O	U	L	M	A	T	E		E	L	I	J	A	H
I	R	S		A	X	E	D		B	I	T			
T	A	L	E	S		C	A	N	O	E		O	A	F
S	L	E	U	T	H		T	A	X	D	O	D	G	E
		R	E	E	F	E	R			N	O	U	N	
A	S	F	O	R	M	E		C	A	T	E	R	E	D
R	E	A	P		A	I	S	L	E	S				
C	A	R	E	L	E	S	S		F	A	E	R	I	E
H	M	M		O	N	T	O	P		S	C	O	T	S
		A	R	E		T	O	T	E		A	S	P	
S	I	S	T	E	R		O	U	T	S	I	D	E	R
I	D	L	I	N	G		P	R	Y		L	I	L	I
T	A	Y	T	A	Y		E	S	L		L	E	F	T

13 PRESENT COMPANY INCLUDED

S	P	A	T		J	A	I	L		C	A	S	T	S
P	U	R	E		A	C	R	E		A	L	T	O	N
A	L	M	A		D	I	E	S	E	L	F	U	E	L
I	P	A		F	E	D		S	A	L	A	D		
N	I	N	J	A			A	E	R	O		F	A	M
	T	I	E	R	R	A	D	E	L	F	U	E	G	O
		W	E	I	R	D			F	R	E	E	S	
D	E	M	I		B	E	E	T	S		A	S	S	T
A	M	I	S	H		D	R	A	W	N				
M	I	C	H	E	L	F	O	U	C	A	U	L	T	
N	T	H		R	O	A	N			N	S	A	I	D
		I	S	A	A	C		B	I	D		U	T	E
A	N	G	E	L	F	A	L	L	S		E	R	A	S
B	E	A	R	D		D	E	E	P		L	I	N	K
C	O	N	E	S		E	D	D	Y		F	E	S	S

14 YULE BE HEARING FROM ME

S	L	O		Z	A	P	P	E	D		R	A	Y	S
M	E	A		U	S	U	R	E	R		A	N	K	A
H	O	R	A	C	E	R	E	L	A	T	I	O	N	S
			S	C	A	R	Y		M	E	N	T	O	S
F	L	A	S	H		S	C	A	R		H	W	Y	
C	I	A		I	S	A		A	S	I	D	E		
C	T	R		N	Y	L	O	N		O	R	C		
	H	O	M	I	N	G	D	Y	N	A	S	T	Y	
	E	N	O		O	D	O	R	S		I	N	N	
		S	T	A	R	R		N	A	B		M	I	A
A	D	O		S	U	E	D		E	L	E	C	T	
B	I	R	T	H	S		I	A	M	S	O			
H	O	K	E	Y	S	I	G	N	A	T	U	R	E	S
O	D	I	N		I	D	U	N	N	O		A	G	O
R	E	N	T		A	S	P	E	N	S		H	O	S

15 RING IN THE NEW YEAR

16 MIDDLE GROUND

17 OFF TO A ROARING START

18 "SEE YOU LATER, ALLIGATOR!"

19 ALUMINUM-INATING

20 OFF TO A GOOD START

21 SWITCH POSITIONS

```
T H I S   S C I F I   H I P S
A U R A   T A P E D   A C A I
X M E N   O M A N I   L Y N X
      J O N O S S O F F
G R O O V E   M I C R O N
R E U S E   P R O   C A I N E
A F T E R N O O N C O F F E E
T E E   A P N E A   F A D
E R R A N D   M E A S L Y
    N A I L   S E L L
C O N T R A C T O F F E R
A L A   W H O   R I G
W I S H B O N E O F F E N S E
O N E R O U S   P E R D I E M
L E S S O R   W A T E R S
```

22 "ALL YOU NEED IS LOVE"

```
B O M B   G L O P   T S A R
O R E E   R E A R   F O U L S
X E N A   A N T I   O R B I T
Y O U C A N T H U R R Y 0
    O N O   S O O
0 H A N D L E S   I N K S A C
H A L   A L T O   C E L L O
O D I S T   A O K   E B O O K
U T T E R   N O R A   M O E
R O O T E R   L A B O R O F 0
    A C E   S W E
0 I S A N O P E N D O O R
I T S T O   A M E N   I S L E
M O U R N   C A L C   A L A N
E M M Y   T R E E   L O F T
```

```
D I A N A   N O L T E   A T M
R O B E S   O D E O N   C H I
J U S T K I D D I N G   R E S
    S O U L   C O W S
L A M P   W H Y B A B Y W H Y
I G U A N A   E S T A D O
B E L L O   I T M E
S E M I M I N O R A X I S
    D U C K   M O V E D
  B I T E M E   G S U I T S
D E C L A S S I F Y   T E S T
I M A C   D I R E
N O R   H E L L T O T H E N O
K A L   A Z T E C   C O V E T
A N Y   Y E E S H   H E A D S
```

23 YOUNG AT HEART

24 ORIGIN STORY

25 INDIVIDUAL RIGHTS

26 IT'S NOT EASY BEING 39-ACROSS

27 COVER ALL THE BASES

28 KIN SELECTION

29 SPOKEN WORD GENRES

30 GEM CLASS

```
P E E R ◇  P E S O S   M R B
A L L A H   E X A C T   I A L
P I A N O   R A S T A   N I A
P E N D U L U M S   B R O N C
    O S E   S Y S   E R I K
A F C W E S T   C A B I N ◇
M O O N   V E R A W A N G
A R M   D I A M O N D   G O O
  O F F A N D O N   P I U S
◇ P O I N T   S E C A N T S
M E R V   L A D   S L R
I N T E R   S Y S T O L I C ◇
N E E   E F I L E   T A C I T
E R R   S U D A N   H Y E N A
R S S   T R E N T   O S T E R
```

31 TELL ME THE BACKSTORY

```
O P R A H   P O N D   G R I P
F L A M E   E C H O   A U R A
T A T T L E T A L E   U D O N
E N O   D U E L   A G E N T
N O N N A R R A T I V E
    O J O S   A M I D A L A
P L A T O   S P A   G O P
F A C E B O O K A C C O U N T
F I R   S P Y   A N A I S
T R E A C L E   W I S K
  G L O C K E N S P I E L
S T O R E   A I R E   D R I
U R G E   S E C R E T P L O T
R A R E   A G E D   T H E S E
E Y E S   Y O Y O   E I D E R
```

32 KITCHEN ISLANDS

```
H B C U   R A C K S   A G A R
E R O S   A C H O O   B I D E
P I S T A C H I O S   E V E R
C O M E L Y   P A N T E N E
A C I D S   P R A D A   M I A
T H C   O B O E S   B L E N D
S E E R   L L C   T O S S E S
  X I A O L O N G B A O
R E P O S T   V I I   T M B G
A M A T I   D E L F T   E R A
T I N   A D O R E   A S S A M
A R S E N I C   Y U P P I E
T A I L   M E L B A T O A S T
A T O M   E N T E R   I C E E
T E N S   S T E E D   L E S S
```

33 MAY FIRST

34 BULL SESSION

35 HEAVY METAL

36 LETTER SHAPES

37 MAKE IT A DOUBLE

38 HEAD GAMES

39 PLACEHOLDERS

40 I'M UP

41 MANE EVENT

Puzzle 39 (top-left grid):

L	A	W	S	■	A	M	A	H	L	■	E	M	T	S
E	L	I	A	■	M	A	L	I	A	■	G	E	R	I
A	L	L	M	Y	P	R	E	T	T	Y	O	N	E	S
F	A	M	O	U	S	■	■	H	I	A	T	U	S	■
■	H	A	A	R	■	U	C	O	N	N	■			
		T	E	N	S	M	A	C	H	I	N	E		
R	I	S	K	■	F	O	I	E	■	E	A	T	E	N
E	N	L	I	S	T	■	■	M	Y	W	O	R	D	
S	C	O	T	T	■	A	M	M	O	■	N	O	D	S
T	H	E	H	U	N	D	R	E	D	S	■			
■	■	C	O	A	S	T	■	O	S	H	A			
■	R	E	A	C	T	S	■	■	O	T	H	E	R	S
C	A	S	T	O	F	T	H	O	U	S	A	N	D	S
A	P	P	T	■	A	R	O	A	R	■	K	N	O	T
M	A	N	Y	■	R	A	N	K	S	■	E	A	R	S

Puzzle 40 (Placeholders grid):

I	M	S	O	B	O	R	E	D	■	P	I	L	S
N	U	T	R	I	T	I	V	E	■	E	C	O	N
F	R	A	N	G	I	P	A	N	I	■	T	H	R	U
I	D	I	O	M	S	■	D	I	L	L	■	O	R	G
R	E	N	T	A	■	P	E	E	L	E	■	R	A	N
M	R	S	■	M	I	R	■	S	W	A	B	B	I	E
■	■	F	A	C	E	D	■	A	P	R	O	N	S
C	O	I	L	■	O	Y	V	E	Y	■	A	Y	E	S
A	P	P	I	A	N	■	D	U	N	E	S	■
S	T	A	T	U	T	E	■	R	E	X	■	O	L	D
H	I	D	■	R	O	D	E	O	■	A	S	P	E	R
S	O	B	■	A	S	I	F	■	S	M	U	T	T	Y
A	N	A	L	■	S	T	I	L	L	I	R	I	S	E
L	A	C	E	■	E	L	A	I	N	E	M	A	Y
E	L	K	S	■	D	E	S	P	E	R	A	T	E

Puzzle 41 (Mane Event grid):

G	O	B	A	D	■	D	I	L	L	S	■	H	A	S
A	T	O	N	E	■	A	D	E	P	T	■	A	C	T
L	I	O	N	E	L	M	E	S	S	I	■	I	R	A
A	S	K	■	P	E	P	S	■	■	F	A	K	E	R
■	■	C	A	D	G	E	■	M	O	L	L	U	S	K
B	I	L	L	I	O	N	A	I	R	E	S	■
A	B	U	T	S	■	L	D	S	■	O	V	E	N
J	I	B	■	H	E	L	L	I	O	N	■	A	X	E
A	S	S	T	■	M	A	I	■	H	A	R	P	O
■	■	R	U	M	R	E	B	E	L	L	I	O	N
F	A	J	I	T	A	S	■	L	A	D	L	E
A	L	A	M	O	■	P	U	R	R	■	T	O	T
Z	I	P	■	P	R	I	D	E	P	A	R	A	D	E
E	V	A	■	I	O	T	A	S	■	F	E	L	I	X
D	E	N	■	A	N	T	S	Y	■	T	V	S	E	T

43 NOTHING BUT NET

42 WHERE IT'S AT

44 OUTGROUPS

45 SNAP OUT OF IT!

46 STATE DEPT.

47 DOUBLE BLOW

A	L	F	A	■	W	A	V	Y	■	S	T	Y	L	E
M	I	L	D	■	E	X	E	S	■	A	H	E	A	D
P	S	I	S	T	I	L	L	L	O	V	E	Y	O	U
S	A	G	■	O	R	E	O	■	N	O	S	E	S	■
■	■	H	O	W	D	■	U	T	E	R	I	■	■	■
P	L	T	R	A	V	E	R	S	■	■	S	L	A	G
A	L	L	E	W	I	S	■	T	L	C	■	I	M	P
N	A	E	■	A	B	C	■	R	O	Z	■	Q	B	S
I	M	S	■	Y	E	A	■	A	S	A	R	U	L	E
C	A	S	A	■	■	P	J	P	A	R	T	I	E	S
■	■	I	M	P	E	I	■	L	I	E	D	■	■	■
■	T	H	R	O	E	■	N	A	A	N	■	D	Y	E
P	I	A	P	P	R	O	X	I	M	A	T	I	O	N
A	D	I	O	S	■	D	I	D	O	■	W	E	N	D
N	E	R	D	Y	■	E	T	A	S	■	O	T	I	S

48 GETTING WARMER

49 FLYING COLORS

L	E	N	D	■	■	T	H	E	N	■	A	S	P	S
I	M	E	A	N	■	A	B	B	Y	■	S	K	I	T
P	O	W	D	E	R	R	O	O	M	■	T	Y	P	O
■	■	■	B	R	O	S	■	■	L	E	G	O	M	E	N
K	A	B	O	O	M	■	H	A	T	E	R	A	D	E
A	T	A	D	■	A	M	P	■	S	T	I	R	■	■
R	O	B	S	■	N	A	S	A	■	M	A	S	T	S
A	N	Y	■	R	O	Y	A	L	W	E	■	H	I	T
T	E	M	P	O	■	A	U	T	O	■	P	A	N	E
■	■	O	H	O	K	■	C	O	O	■	O	L	G	A
I	N	N	O	T	I	M	E	■	H	O	U	S	E	D
S	U	I	T	S	M	E	■	T	O	A	T	■	■	■
L	E	T	O	■	B	L	U	E	O	R	I	G	I	N
A	V	O	N	■	R	O	S	E	■	S	N	A	R	E
M	A	R	S	■	A	N	O	N	■	■	E	Y	E	D

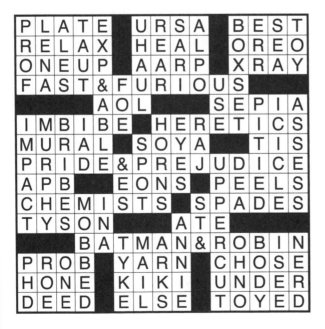

P	L	A	T	E	■	U	R	S	A	■	B	E	S	T
R	E	L	A	X	■	H	E	A	L	■	O	R	E	O
O	N	E	U	P	■	A	A	R	P	■	X	R	A	Y
F	A	S	T	&	F	U	R	I	O	U	S	■	■	■
■	■	■	A	O	L	■	■	S	E	P	I	A	■	■
I	M	B	I	B	E	■	H	E	R	E	T	I	C	S
M	U	R	A	L	■	S	O	Y	A	■	■	T	I	S
P	R	I	D	E	&	P	R	E	J	U	D	I	C	E
A	P	B	■	E	O	N	S	■	P	E	E	L	S	■
C	H	E	M	I	S	T	S	■	S	P	A	D	E	S
T	Y	S	O	N	■	■	A	T	E	■	■	■	■	■
■	■	B	A	T	M	A	N	&	R	O	B	I	N	■
P	R	O	B	■	Y	A	R	N	■	C	H	O	S	E
H	O	N	E	■	K	I	K	I	■	U	N	D	E	R
D	E	E	D	■	E	L	S	E	■	T	O	Y	E	D

50 DOUBLE FEATURES

100

51 ON/OFF THE CLOCK

52 FREE JAZZ

53 BROKEN CLOCK

101

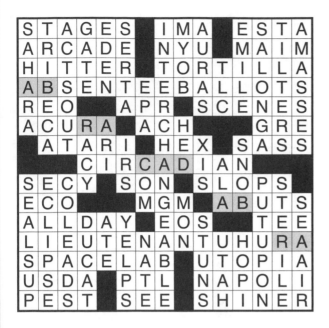

54 DOWNCAST

55 HOUSE EXPANSION

56 CAN'T LOSE

57 THE SILENCE OF THE LAMBS

58 THAT SOUNDS SPOOOOKY!

59 YOU'RE STARTING TO SCARE ME AGAIN!

61 SERVICE CENTER

62 PAST, PRESENT, AND FUTURE

63 THE WORST THANKSGIVING EVER!

64 VIBE CHECK

65 SOUNDS COOL!

67 SOLVING FOR X-MAS

66 'TIS THE SEASON

68 SWITCHING SIDES

K	I	T	E		S	O	N	A	T	A		I	R	A
I	R	O	N		L	E	A	K	E	D		N	O	R
W	I	N	D	S	O	R	T	I	E	S		L	U	C
I	S	S	U	E			C	M	S		O	A	T	H
			S	W	A	S	H	B	U	C	K	L	E	
A	N	T	E	N	N	A		O	P	E	R	A		
B	U	R	R		T	I	P			D	A	L	E	S
E	D	U		W	I	L	D	R	Y	E		A	T	E
T	E	M	P	O			T	O	O		A	N	N	A
	P	R	O	A	M		A	G	E	N	D	A	S	
S	C	A	F	F	O	L	D	I	N	G				
A	W	A	Y		F	D	A		V	E	N	U	S	
H	E	R		L	A	U	N	D	R	Y	L	I	S	T
O	D	D		O	I	L	C	A	N		I	N	D	Y
Y	E	S		B	R	E	E	D	S		C	O	A	X

69 GET A LOAD OF THIS!

70 BLOOD DONOR

J	A	M		R	B	I	S		F	I	B	U	L	A
A	T	A		O	O	N	A		A	D	O	N	I	S
D	O	Y	O	U	W	A	N	T	T	O	A	B	E	T
E	M	A	I	L	S		D	I	E	T		L	U	I
		L	E	T	S	I	N		O	L	E			
G	O	T		T	O	E		Y	O	U	A	L	L	
S	T	O	A	T		C	O	T	E		N	C	A	A
P	R	O	P	E	R	T	Y	B	R	I	G	H	T	S
O	A	T	H		O	S	L	O		M	E	E	T	S
T	S	H	I	R	T		N	A	P		D	E	O	
	F	D	A		P	A	E	L	L	A				
M	A	A		T	E	R	N		T	A	C	O	M	A
O	M	I	S	S	I	O	N	C	O	N	T	R	O	L
T	E	R	R	O	R		I	N	I	T		C	A	P
T	R	Y	O	N	E		E	N	D	S		A	B	O

T	A	N		S	I	B	S		E	M	P	T	Y
M	A	D	E		A	R	Y	A		L	Y	D	I	A
E	R	I	E		C	I	R	C	L	E	B	A	C	K
D	I	E	D		H	S	N		A	M	A	S	S	
S	Q	U	A	R	E	H	E	A	D	E	D			
		H	A	T			G	I	N		S	P	F	
C	O	P	A	Y		T	O	E	T	O	T	O	E	
A	N	O	N		V	L	O	G	S		V	A	N	S
B	L	U	D	G	E	O	N			F	E	N	D	S
S	Y	R		O	L	D		W	A	R				
	L	O	V	E	T	R	I	A	N	G	L	E	
S	W	E	D	E		I	O	N		I	R	O	N	
T	H	E	O	C	T	A	G	O	N		G	I	R	D
B	E	A	N	O		Y	E	T	I		H	E	R	O
A	D	R	E	P		E	R	S	E		T	R	Y	

71 GETTING IN SHAPE

72 LOOK INSIDE

73 PLAYING DOUBLES

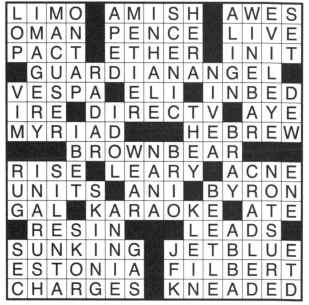

74 ABOUT FACE

75 CAN I HAVE YOUR DIGITS?

76 DISAMBIGUATION

77 INSURANCE CARRIERS

78 THE NAME GAME

79 LET THE UPSETS BEGIN

80 CRITICAL THINKING

81 RETRO SHADES

82 MUSICAL TRIO

83 TAX SEASON

84 WHOA THERE!

85 BUSINESS FORMATION